CW01496724

The Necessary Step

Cataloguing to Recognise and Enhance the Value of School Heritage

Edited by

Marta Brunelli and Francesca Davida Pizzigoni

The Necessary Step: Cataloguing to Recognise and Enhance the Value of School Heritage

Edited by Marta Brunelli and Francesca Davida Pizzigoni

2025

Ethics International Press, UK

British Library Cataloguing in Publication Data

A catalogue record for this book is available from the British Library

Copyright © 2025 by the Editors and Contributors

All rights for this book reserved. No part of this book may be reproduced, stored in a retrieval system, or transmitted, in any form or by any means, electronic, mechanical, photocopying, recording or otherwise, without the prior permission of the copyright owner.

ISBN (Hardback): 978-1-83711-100-8

ISBN (Ebook): 978-1-83711-101-5

The translation of this work has been funded by SEPS
SEGRETARIATO EUROPEO PER LE PUBBLICAZIONI SCIENTIFICHE

SEGRETARIATO EUROPEO PER LE PUBBLICAZIONI SCIENTIFICHE

www.seps.it - seps@seps.it

Translated by

Antonella Di Pasquale

Table of Contents

Preface: The Necessary Step and the Open Challenges for Safeguarding and Enhancing School Heritage

Anna Ascenzi

In recent years, there has been a real historiographical revolution, which has given life to new lines of research in the historical-educational field. In fact, as it is known, in 1995 the French historian Dominique Julia proposed to consider school culture as "the set of norms, which define the knowledge to be taught and the behaviours to be inculcated, as well as the educational practices, which allow their correct transmission and assimilation by the recipients of the educational action" (Julia 1995a). By introducing it as a historical object of investigation, Julia assigned a prominent role to the history of school subjects, as it was able to describe the dynamics that take place within the school classroom. In the wake of this reflection, a new approach to writing the history of education and schooling has emerged.

Over the past thirty years, scholars have paid particular attention to the material culture of schooling, and, at the same time, there has been a growing interest in the protection and safeguard of this rich historical-educational heritage not only by institutions linked to the academic field, but also by private individuals, schools, national and local bodies and administrations. As a result, museums, historical halls and collections of specific objects were created and study days and opportunities for discussion involving educational historians, but also the school world and other realities,

which were engaged in collecting, enhancing and studying historical-educational heritage, were organised[1].

In 2004, the development of studies and research on the historical-educational heritage favoured the birth of Sociedad Española
para el Estudio del Patrimonio Histórico-Educativo (SEPHE),
which started engaging in the protection and conservation of
historical-educational heritage, studying and searching for this
heritage and the promotion, support and dissemination of actions
linked to the above-mentioned purposes among its fundamental
goals. On September 13th, 2017, Società Italiana per lo studio del
Patrimonio Storico-Educativo was officially born.[2] Following the
model of this society – and of other similar academic and scientific
associations that have emerged in recent years in Portugal, France,
Switzerland, and Latin America (Brazil, Argentina, Chile, Mexico,
etc.) – the Società Italiana per lo Studio del Patrimonio Storico-Educativo was officially established on 13 September 2017, on the
initiative of research groups in the history of education active at
twelve Italian universities (Roma Tre, Florence, Macerata, Molise,

---

[1]   As a demonstration of the strong attention paid to the historical-educa-
      tional heritage not only by the academic scientific community, but also by
      private individuals, schools, national and local bodies and administrations,
      it is highlighted that "Società Italiana per lo Studio del Patrimonio Stori-
      co-Educativo" has also received a support coming from educational insti-
      tutions and school educational museums since its creation. Furthermore,
      the second congress, which was organised by SIPSE – and held in Padua on
      7th and 8th October 2021 –, saw the participation of educational historians,
      but also school headmasters, teachers coming from schools of all levels,
      representatives of historical institutes and archivists. For further informa-
      tion, see the acts of the congress Ascenzi, Covato and Zago (2021).

[2]   SIPSE was born as part of the III *International Conference on School Material
      Culture* «Production, Use and Circulation of School Furnishings and Teach-
      ing Aids between Europe and Latin America in XIX and XX Centuries»,
      which was held at the University of Macerata on 12th and 13th September
      2017. About SIPSE creation see Brunelli (2017).

Bari, Foggia, Bologna, Basilicata, Calabria, Padua, Bolzano, and the Catholic University of Milan).

Since the beginning, the Italian Society has set itself to protect, preserve and enhance the historical-educational heritage at educational museums, documentation and research centres on historical-educational heritage, historical schools and, more generally, schools of all levels. Furthermore, it is committed to promoting local hubs for the survey, collection, and cataloguing of this heritage and to protect the national (librarian, archival, architectural or museum) historical-educational heritage, promoting initiatives, which are aimed at avoiding its dispersion and deterioration, also through an appropriate reporting to the competent authorities. In addition, SIPSE's activities also include the development of specific protocols for the conservation of school cultural heritage, defining its cataloguing criteria and preparing guidelines and complementary tools to be distributed in schools of all levels, the development of interest in school heritage by the school world and, more generally, civil society, highlighting its teaching and popular functions, the promotion of agreements among various participating institutions in order to facilitate exchanges of information, practices and experiences, as well as the development of common programs and shared regulations. Finally, it is important for society to create connections with similar foreign associations. In fact, since its creation, SIPSE has had an authentically international vocation, considering the discussion on every aspect, which is fundamental with the studies on historical-educational heritage carried out in various countries and with methodologies, sources, lines of investigation and historiographical approaches[4]. This is a very important aspect, as it allows the Society to broaden its research perspectives in fact, the Society intends to strengthen cohesion, comparison and collaboration with the international network of scholars.

Among the most important goals of the Italian Scientific Society is the creation of a European network of academic societies engaged in the study of historical educational heritage, but also the valorisation of young scholars and the promotion of highly specialised studies and research through the series «Thesaurus Scholae. Sources and studies on school heritage», which is organised into two distinct sections, "Studies" and "Sources". The "Studies" section is destined to have the acts of the conferences and the seminars, which are promoted by SIPSE, as well as monographic volumes by individual scholars and collective volumes containing Italian and foreign scholars' contributions relating to studies and research on historical-educational heritage[3]. Instead, the "Sources" section includes the results of the censuses for school heritage and welfare and educational institutions for children and young people in our country, which were carried out at a local and regional level.

In May 2020, four thematic work committees for school and educational movable properties, which were composed of some members of the society, were precisely created to make SIPSE mission even more incisive and effective. Thus, there was the *work committee for School Archives*, which aims at examining the problems and the potential relating to school archives as sources for the history of education to be known, preserved and valorised as school heri-

---

[3]   The first SIPSE congress was held in Palma de Mallorca, Spain, from 20th to 23rd November 2018, in conjunction with the celebration of the VIII Jornadas Científicas de la Sociedad Española para el Estudio del Patrimonio Histórico-Educativo (SEPHE), the homologous Spanish Scientific Society to which the Italian Society is linked by solid and profitable collaborative relationships at an international level. Please, see the acts of the Congress edited by Ascenzi, Covato and Meda (2020).

tage, the *work committee for School Libraries and School Book Heritage*, which is engaged in the recognition of what exists in Italy as the first medium-term goal, starting, first of all, from the individual realities where the components of the committee are acting, the *work committee for School Museums and School Scientific collections*, whose main goal is the census of school heritage in museums, and the *work committee for Cataloguing School Heritage*, which has the intrinsic goal of working towards the definition of criteria for cataloguing school heritage[4]. The committees created a census form for the historical-educational heritage and are keeping on working on the bibliographic recognition of studies and research, which are devoted to a specific topic, the recognition of any experiences on censuses and teaching activities, which have already started at a local level, and the definition of a kit of good practices.

Therefore, this volume is placed within the research activities by the SIPSE and the work of its thematic committees, specifically the *Committee for Cataloguing School Heritage*. This is a committee whose main goal is to arrive at the definition of criteria for cataloguing school heritage, which are currently without any uniformly recognised rules, directions, or cataloguing protocols. Therefore, the final goal will be to achieve the promotion of a cataloguing card for the historical-educational heritage to be submitted to Istituto Centrale per il Catalogo e la Documentazione belonging to the Italian Ministry of Culture. This ambitious operation intrinsically contains a further essential goal: to achieve the official recognition of the "School heritage" category.

---

[4] The mandate program was published in minutes no. 1 of the Governing Council meeting of June 15th, 2018, and can be consulted in the register of minutes: <http://www.sipse.eu/wpcontent/uploads/2022/11/Consiglio-Direttivo_Registro-dei-verbali.pdf> (24.01.2023).

This is a considerable challenge precisely since "school heritage" has not enjoyed a specific legal recognition up to now. Consequently, this is a heritage category with loose and sometimes subjective boundaries and all the consequences, which this lack of definition brings with it. For this reason, the committee felt the need to work in a plural direction, which is able to identify and face some of these complexities, trying to offer a contribution not only to discussion on specific topics, but also to suggest possible solutions.

To achieve these two macro-goals, the Committee aims to start a comparative analysis of the existing cataloguing cards, which are recognized by ICCD today and referred to those kinds of heritage – such as, for example, technical-scientific collections – within which a part of school heritage can be traced back, drawing up a list of materials, which are part of the "School heritage" category to arrive at a single and unambiguously recognized definition of the assets belonging to this kind of heritage and identifying its possible categories and subcategories and studying the teaching implications of the cataloguing operations for school heritage as its first actions[5].

The necessary step: cataloguing to enhance school heritage collects the results of these first reflections and is divided into essays, which are devoted to a single specific matter of the macro-topic "cataloguing", considering it in the broadest possible sense.

The first chapter *A heritage in search of protection. Ideas and reflections for a potential category of "school heritage"* by Marta Brunelli together

---

[5] See the website page of the Work committee for cataloguing school heritage: <http://www.sipse.eu/commissione-di-lavoro-sulla-catalogazione-dei-beni-culturali-della-scuola/> (11.03.2023).

with Carmen Vitale, resumes and updates the previous essay written ten years ago by Brunelli (2013) who had had the merit of being one of the first to draw attention to the lack of specific categorisation of school heritage. That essay offered a review of the Italian legislation relating to cultural assets from a legal point of view, paying attention to the fact that we were still faced with "a category to be defined" with respect to school-related assets. Furthermore, it underlined how this indeterminacy inevitably affected the possibility of creating a rigorous and scientific cataloguing of this heritage category. Now, ten years after that groundbreaking work, Brunelli and Vitale intend to offer an update of the reflection, identifying any regulatory steps forward and trying to specify useful elements to arrive at a more necessary definition of the heritage category on which the possibility of a correct conservation and valorisation of school heritage depends.

In their essay Mara Orlando and Valeria Viola *How to catalogue a school heritage? Reflections and first results* reflect on the national cataloguing system, which is regulated by ICCD. In the absence of a scientifically coherent and officially validated descriptive standard for historical school heritage—one approved by the national bodies responsible for coordinating cataloguing activities of cultural heritage at a national level, the two authors get through the different recognized cataloguing cards today by looking for possible "adaptations" of these cards to meet the specific needs of school heritage. The result is a significant comparative analysis of the catalogue templates currently in use at the ICCD for heritage types under which school assets might be classified. Then, the work goes as far as to suggest a solution, which is easily practicable, but very diriment for the issue, identifying the specific Area (the ATB one) in the cataloguing cards, which are currently recognized and included in SIGECweb, as a "paragraph" where to include the belonging indication of an asset to "school heritage", thus allowing to easily identify school materials, even if they are catalogued in cards relating to different kinds of assets.

The essay *Exercise books among research, teaching and third mission. Some reflections in view of a cataloguing card* by Francesca Borruso considers the specific school heritage represented by the school exercise book. It is analysed in its peculiar features, including its study in the context of the attention it has garnered within historical-educational research in recent years. Recognising the needs arising from different research perspectives, Borruso presents some proposals for cataloguing exercise books. These proposals suggest a possible cataloguing card that takes into account the inherent peculiarity of this cultural asset: an object, yet also a container of traces of school life.

The following two chapters delve beyond the strictly historiographical approach to explore the pedagogical applications of cataloguing activities in the classroom, examining their ability to directly engage students and unlock the fullest pedagogical potential of the school heritage.

In *Observing and describing objects. Cataloguing as a method for learning in schoolwork* Marta Brunelli offers a framework for the theoretical and methodological references of this approach. In fact, if scientific cataloguing can be considered as the final act of a whole series of study, understanding and classification actions for an asset, then these actions can be fully considered as essential phases of the process itself and can be investigated with respect to their didactic-educational potential. After identifying the historical-pedagogical roots of this approach, the essay highlights the skills on which this kind of activity can have an impact: from observation to learning to the formulation of hypotheses, description, representation, classification. In other words, the essay intends to show how the cataloguing activity, when changed into a "heritage description" to be developed in the classroom, can be fully considered a teaching strategy.

In the final essay *Pedagogical cataloguing: proposing initial cataloguing activities to be linked to school activities*, jointly written by Marta Brunelli and Francesca Davida Pizzigoni, a review is offered of the first experiences developed in Italy that adopted this pedagogical vision of the cataloguing of school heritage. The valorisation of these experiences starts from the belief that a fundamental step is achieved through careful and dedicated study, manipulation, observation, and direct contact: from a student, who is a simple user of the heritage or a distracted observer, to an aware student, who becomes a protagonist of knowledge and interpretation of the heritage. This represents a clear change of position and role. The students take up the role of co-builders of knowledge and, consequently, of responsible future advocates. Therefore, the article reconstructs the experiences of *La Scuola è il Nostro Patrimonio*, the Turin school museum network, the practice of "Patrimonieri" and the NEMO project of the Neapolitan Historical Schools, highlighting their teaching approaches and making worksheets available.

In short, the volume represents the first systematic work entirely devoted to the topic of cataloguing historical-educational heritage. It has the ability to face the topic from various points of view, highlighting the aspect of the legal recognition of this heritage category, the needs for institutionally recognized cataloguing cards for these assets, the peculiarities of some assets within this category, without neglecting a more didactic-educational approach of cataloguing practice. Therefore, the merit is not only concentrating on the topic, such as the often-sloppy cataloguing of school heritage, but also combining different research perspectives that are able to take into account different needs, purposes and possibilities with respect to the macro-topic of "cataloguing". The work does not limit itself to focusing on them, but seeks to offer solutions and strategies, opening up the field for future research developments.

Therefore, this volume undoubtedly represents an achievement as it is able to put together the work carried out by the members of the committee in recent years and to fill a significant gap on the topic of school heritage but, at the same time, this is a starting point to launch further interesting initiatives and relevant studies and research with the aim of spreading and strengthening that sensitivity towards the recovery, valorisation and study of school heritage. These actions represent not only a benefit for educational historians, but also for teachers and students, who will be able to undertake innovative paths on teaching history within schools using historical-educational heritage. Such initiatives offer valuable experiences of heritage education, particularly for younger generations. Through them, students can gain knowledge of the past and, in turn, contribute to the protection and promotion of the historical educational heritage — ensuring it is not forgotten or lost.

Introduction: The Committee for Cataloguing School Heritage

Francesca Davida Pizzigoni

The activities of the Committee for Cataloguing School Heritage started in May 2020 as part of the Italian Society for Research on Historical-Educational Heritage (SIPSE) and, specifically, as the Society's desire to launch four thematic work committees[6]. The specific task of our committee[7] is already intrinsic in its name: deeply examining the possibilities of arriving at the definition of criteria for cataloguing historical-educational heritage. In fact, as it is known (Brunelli 2013), there have been no uniformly and institutionally recognized rules, directions or cataloguing protocols with respect to this category of heritage[8] in Italy up to now. Consequently, the priority goal towards which the Committee oriented has been to carry out an in-depth study since the beginning of its activities to fill this gap.

As regards the Italian context, the cataloguing of school heritage, in order to be recognised from a legal-administrative point of view, should be carried out through the SIGECweb, the General

---

[6] These are the Work Committee for School Archives; the Work Committee for school museums and school science collections; the work committee for school libraries and schoolbook heritage; the Work Committee for cataloguing school heritage.

[7] The Committee, coordinated by me, is composed of Marta Brunelli (University of Macerata), Francesca Borruso (University of Roma Tre), Mara Orlando (University of Padua) and Valeria Viola ("Giustino Fortunato" University).

[8] About the categorization of school heritage and their conservation, please see also Meda (2010 and 2013).

Cataloguing Information System developed by the Ministry for Cultural Heritage. This tool obviously uses only the cataloguing cards issued by the Central Institute for the Catalogue and Documentation (ICCD) belonging to the Italian Ministry of Culture. Consequently, the final goal, which the Committee sets, is to promote a cataloguing card for the Historical Educational Heritage within this ICCD Institute. This ambitious operation holds a further essential goal: to achieve an official recognition of the "school heritage" category, which is not often uniquely identified today or, in any case, without certain boundaries. As we know well, failure to identify which assets are part of this heritage category leads to inevitable (and irreversible) consequences up to the loss of the heritage itself.

In other words, it's clear that unambiguously identifying any school asset as part of a heritage and cataloguing it through its own data is a fundamental step. This enables us to safeguard the asset, then locate, examine, and correlate it with other assets, delving into its deepest significance.

To achieve these two macro-objectives (i.e. to define which items belong to the category of historical-educational heritage and to have a specific cataloguing card that identifies them as part of this heritage category from a legal-administrative point of view), the Committee embarked on a step-by-step research process as its first medium-term action. This gradual process aimed to first analyze the 'problem' and consider its various aspects Once these aspects had been identified, the aim was to initiate an assessment of the status quo for each of them, by collecting and analysing legislation, national and international experiences and the possibilities for intervention. This would then lead to the formulation of initial proposals for possible solutions, or at least long-term strategies.

Following this approach, as a result of the first action for a "problem study", it was therefore established:

to start a comparative analysis of the existing cataloguing cards today, which are recognized by Istituto Centrale per il Catalogo e la Documentazione and referred to those kinds of heritage (for example, technical-scientific collections) within which a part of school heritage can be traced back, consequently identifying which sub-categories of school heritage are excluded from the current ICCD cataloguing possibilities.

– to draw up a list of materials, which are part of the "School heritage" category, identifying their possible categories and subcategories.

– to study the teaching implications of the cataloguing operations for school heritage.

With respect to the second point, the need to reflect on the current regulatory framework within which this category of assets is included has emerged as a closely related consequence, thus updating a framework study on the process for the legal recognition of school heritage in Italy – exactly ten years after the above-mentioned essay by Brunelli, which was devoted to the topic and a point of reference for the whole study community.

Instead, with respect to the will to specifically deal with teaching strategies and curricular implications of this activity within the Committee, which is devoted to cataloguing school heritage, it arises from considerations, which belong to two different areas. The first one refers to the topic of the conservation and valorisation of historical-educational heritage: in the face of the fact that it is objectively impossible for the research community to directly deal with every reality, it is appropriate to create a widespread community of people, who are sensitive to the topic of histori-cal-educational heritage, since it is so widespread and preserved at each school. In particular, these are pupils, teachers, headmas-ters, school staff and school community in a broad sense (i.e., those who are in daily contact with these assets, which are at school very often) and the added value, which is potentially their ability to recognize and to consequently protect these assets. In our opin-ion, the possibilities of safeguarding a heritage at risk of dispersion are increased through a training action on the knowledge of these assets – which passes through teaching activities in the classroom.

Instead, the second reason refers to various skills for students, which teaching activities based on cataloguing school heritage have expressed in their ability to develop and, therefore, the opportunity for school to see its own heritage as an added value in terms of concrete and positive implications in the curricular course and the application of active and laboratory methodological strat-egies, offering solutions to school needs. Without considering that the more school heritage are perceived by school as a value and a response to its daily needs (and not, instead, as an "extra thing" to deal with), the more they will be objects of attention and care by the school community (Pizzigoni 2022c).

Returning to the working paths, which have been dealt with in this first phase of the Committee's life, as the reflection has progressed, it was considered appropriate to devote to in-depth research stud-ies on specific subcategories of school heritage and it was decided to start from the one represented by a multifaceted and complex asset, which is able to include information related to the artefact (manufacturer, series, format, etc.) as well as its content in it: the historical exercise books.

Now, this volume intends to collect the results of these first reflection goals, which the Committee had set.

In this preface – which is a narrative of how our Committee understood the mandate received and how it tried to develop it in this first period of activity –, it seems significant to share a coincidence, which questioned and struck us a lot: this reflection works on the topic of cataloguing school heritage (which brings the implications of safeguarding, protecting and valorising it, as it is mentioned) precisely developed in coincidence with the pandemic linked to COVID-19. As is well known, it had a severe and profound impact on every reality, including the school world, which is par excellence the place where a large quantity of historical pedagogical objects is kept, more or less consciously. The difficult moments of school firstly forced its closure and then the return to the classroom with distancing rules led to the need for schools to identify and to reuse different larger spaces where to have lessons. Beyond the priority aspects of safeguarding health and the right to education, our committee naturally found itself reflecting on the fact that this emergency phase and this need for new spaces could represent a moment of particular danger for school heritage. On the one hand, the objective priorities linked to emergency could lead to a natural and understandable less attention towards historical assets, which were preserved at school, and on the other hand, the haste with which school found itself acting in order to find new spaces could lead to a clearance of rooms, which were perhaps useful as a deposit for these assets with the inevitable dispersion of this heritage.

By recalling how SIPSE's sensitivity and its leadership prompted it to offer its own contribution in that emergency context through an open letter, aimed at supporting the school world in considering these aspects[9], the coincidence between the pandemic and the start of our study activities on cataloguing school heritage made us reflect on the fragility of this heritage once again, in an even more poignant way. This led us to feel the *urgency* of having a framework for the recognition and protection of this category of heritage, even more clearly, if possible. Therefore, we intended to work considering the aspect of cataloguing these assets as an essential and "necessary" preliminary action – to use the term that SIPSE President Anna Ascenzi well identified when referring to this step. Therefore, we owned this adjective associated with the step, which is constituted by cataloguing, in the awareness that assets have no identity without cataloguing: they do not have a name, a location, or a date.

In other words, *they don't exist*. There are no legally valid lists (we don't even call them real inventories!), there are no univocal criteria, which make them immediately recognized as a heritage and, moreover, attributable to a specific category of heritage with its specific features. But they *don't* really *exist* in a broader sense, that is, they will always be "dispersible".

The Committee's intended effort is to shed light on what we can identify as a real need, considering cataloguing as a crucial step towards achieving protection (through full recognition) and considering protection as a tool to enable the entire community not only to to share this heritage in the present and future, but also to preserve the fundamental research object related to the field of investigation on school materiality for future years.

---

[9]   See the SIPSE open letter of July 17th, 2020 (prot. n. 5.2/U/0023) entitled *Appello alla salvaguardia del patrimonio culturale delle scuole*.

Our committee's contributions are undoubtedly initial and partial solutions and proposals, which can be refined over time. However, we're eager to share them with the entire scientific community, precisely to foster new joint advances and reflections. These will enable us to collectively develop increasingly effective tools for safeguarding, protecting, and enhancing the school heritage.

Chapter 1

A Heritage in Search of Safeguarding: Reflections on the Scientific, Cultural and Legal Framing of a New Category of "School Heritage" [1]

Marta Brunelli and Carmen Vitale

Introduction: an emerging heritage in search of protection

This publication illustrates the main issues that have arisen during the work of the SIPSE Committee for the Cataloguing of School heritage, concerning the definition of descriptive protocols for historical school materials, which are nowadays widely distributed throughout Italy. These materials, in fact, are preserved in different locations: firstly, in schools; secondly, in university research centres dealing with history of education or history of disciplinary teaching and, finally, in all those public or private conservation institutes (museums or museum collections)[2], which collect and

---

[1]   This work is the result of the joint work of two authors; nevertheless, we would like to specify that Marta Brunelli is the author of paragraphs 1, 2 and 3; Carmen Vitale is the author of paragraphs 4 and 5. The authors have revised, updated and extended the essay by Brunelli (2013).

[2]   The distinction between museum and museum collection is explained in international documents, such as the ICOM *Definition of museum* and the ICOM *Code of Ethics* (<https://icom.museum/en/>) or the ICOM publication by Desvallées & Mairesse (2010). The same distinction is found in national

show school objects and documents acquired in various ways and with different purposes.

To understand the wide distribution of the materials discussed here, it may be useful to make the following distinction:

1) Collections and museums whose institutional mission is to collect and preserve this type of objects. In this case, we are talking about real museums of historical-educational heritage, which represent a growing typology in Italy and abroad;

2) Collections and museums containing groups of school materials within collections of a completely different disciplinary nature. This is the case, for example, of ethnographic museums dedicated to the preservation of local traditions and popular culture, which almost always have a section on education or the local school (Pic. 1.1);

3) Collections and museums that preserve school materials used and/or produced by a single school, documenting not only the history of that school but also the evolution

---

legislation: see the definition of museum in Legislative Decree no. 42 of January 22nd, 2004, art. 101 of the Code of Cultural Heritage and Landscape and the Ministerial Decree of May 10th, 2001, *Atto di indirizzo sui criteri tecnico-scientifici e sugli standard di funzionamento e sviluppo dei musei* (<https://www.beniculturali.it/mibac/multimedia/MiBAC/documents/ 1310746917330_DM10_5_01.pdf> [15.08.2022]). In the latter, a clear distinction is made between museums that "with their own and/or allocated resources, carry out precise integrated functions: conservation of objects and collections, research on them, relevant communication", and collections to which "the function of conservation is primarily assigned" (*ibid.*: Introduction, p. 14). The distinction lies in the accessibility and openness to the public, which is limited in the case of the collection. The same concept is found in various regional systems, which have incorporated the ministerial directive, such as the Decision of the Regional Council no. 809/2009 of the Marche Region.

of teaching practices and the organisation of the Italian school system in relation to a specific school level. While various collections can be found in schools across Italy, true museums are a rarity, but they have been gaining momentum in recent years. A striking case is MITI, *Museo dell'Innovazione e della Tecnica Industriale* (Museum of Industrial Innovation and Technique), located in the historical workshops of the Montani Industrial Technical Institute in Fermo and inaugurated in 2012 (Pic. 1.2).

The need to properly preserve and describe these objects arises from the fact that, in recent years, these material testimonies have been the subject of increasing attention from many figures who, although motivated by different (and complementary) motives and purposes, are now working more and more closely with these historical materials. From their own perspectives, these people have helped to clarify the different levels of meaning and value that school materials embody.

Among those who have demonstrated a significant interest in school materials, we find, first and foremost, historians of education who, following the international evolution of historiographical paradigms, have embarked on new lines of research specifically linked to the material sources of school history. The history of education, particularly school history, can be studied from different perspectives. One is national, such as the evolution of the Italian school system. Another is comparative, examining the development of school systems in various countries. Finally, it can be approached from the perspective of «transnational history», a concept introduced by Diana Gonçalves Vidal (2020). This approach demonstrates how the international circulation of pedagogical ideas, educational practices, and school materials between the 19th and 20th centuries should be reinterpreted not as the history of an assimilation process, but as a polycentric history of numerous cultural appropriation processes carried out by school systems in each national context.

Pic. 1.1 *Reconstruction of a rural classroom inside the Museum of popular culture (in Ponzano di Fermo) a private collection (source: <http://www.museoculturapopolare.it/>, 11.12.2022)*

Pic. 1.2. *The MITI: Museo dell'innovazione e della tecnica industriale (Fermo), the engine room of a former foundry (source: <https://www.museo-miti.it/>, 11.12.2022)*

In addition to historians of education, there is also the growing interest that has emerged in recent years by curators and conservators working in museums specifically dedicated to school heritage. These include public museums managed by local authorities, cultural associations or foundations, such as the *Museum of the School/Schulmuseum* of the City of Bolzano, created in 1993 and opened to the public in 1995[3]; the *Museum of the School* of Pergine, created in 1997 by a group of teachers from "Don Milani" primary school[4]; or the *MUSLI – Museum of the School and Children's Literature*, founded in 2002 in Turin and now an offshoot of the Tancredi di Barolo Foundation – only to mention the most pioneering and significant cases.

Another emerging reality is that of university-based museums, which are more open to the non-academic public. University museums currently operating in Italy are the *MUSED – "Mauro Laeng" Museum of School and Education* at the University of Roma Tre (founded in 1986 and heir to the tradition of the nineteenth-century Museum of Education in Rome), the *Museum of Education* at the University of Padua (established in 1993), the *MUDESC – "Paolo and Ornella Ricca" Museum of the School* at the University of Macerata (created in 2009 and opened to the public in 2012), the *Museum of School and Popular Education* at the University of Molise, was created in 2013, and, finally, the *Permanent Exhibition on the History of the South Tyrolean School*, created in 2007 at the Centre for Research and Documentation on the History of Education in the University of Bressanone, South Tyrol. However, the number and size of school collections is extremely large and only partially

---

[3] See the institutional website at the URL: <http://www.gemeinde.bozen.it/cultura_context.jsp?ID_LINK=751&area=48> (20.10.2022).

[4] See the Institutional website: <http://www.museoscuolapergine.it/it/> (20.10.2022).

known, which is why the research group operating at the University of Macerata has launched a specific census project[5].

In all these contexts, there is a growing need to describe school objects using scientifically based, uniform and, above all, functional criteria for a careful historical recontextualisation. This will allow us to properly appreciate their value and significance as material sources of school history. These material sources are highly heterogeneous, ranging from exercise books to drawings, from teaching aids to writing utensils, from school furniture and furnishings to minor materials such as pupils' equipment, including school bags, stationery, school uniforms, badges, and many other objects. Such diversity raises critical questions. Some are general, concerning the macro-category of 'school materials'. Others are more specific, related to each subtype included within it (Pics. 1.3-5).

---

[5] The Permanent Observatory of Educational Museums and Research Centres on Historical-Educational Heritage (OPeNMuSE) at the University of Macerata, funded in 2011 as a working group inside «Paolo e Ornella Ricca» Museum of the School History, has been officially working since 2014 to carry out a census of museums, research centres and associations active in the preservation, study and valorisation of historical-school heritage in Italy. The map of the Italian museums and the census forms collected so far are available on the web page: <https://www.unimc.it/cescom/it/openmuse> (21.12.2022).

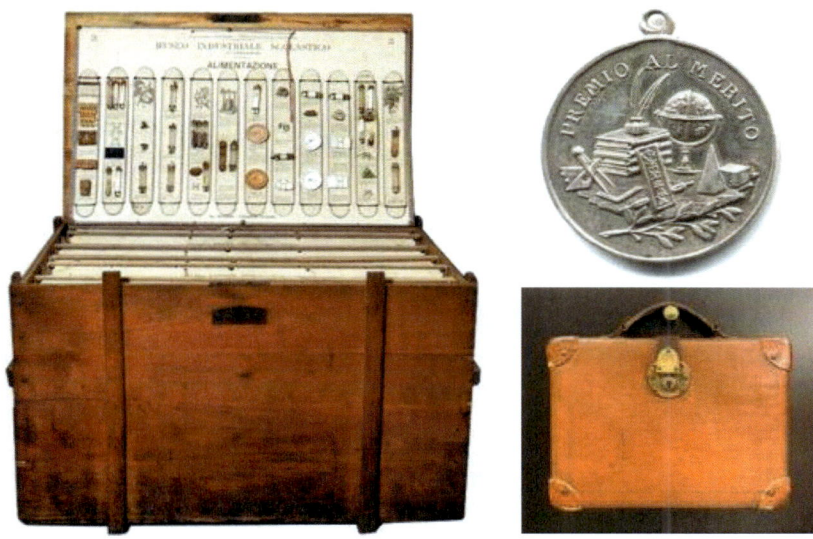

Pic. 1.3. *(on the left) Museo Industriale Scolastico. MUSLI in Turin (source: <https://www.fondazionetancredidibarolo.com/>, 12.09.2022);* **Pic. 1.4**. *(on the top right) School merit medal (n.d. but late 19th century), a private collection (photo by Marta Brunelli);* **Pic. 1.5** *(on the right) Fibre satchel with handle, angles and turn-lock closure. Ca. 1900-1930, MUDESC - Museo della Scuola «Paolo e Ornella Ricca» (photo by Marco Gasparri)*

In addition to historians and museum professionals, teachers are also interested in the problems of conservation, management and accurate description of school materials. This is due to the fact that an increasing number of teachers are using their school's historical materials to develop innovative teaching projects with their pupils, as some of the experiences reported in this volume confirm. This pedagogical and cultural interest reflects international, European and national educational policies which, from the 1990s to the present day, have identified Heritage Education as an active and interdisciplinary teaching method that is particularly flexible and functional for the educational needs of contemporary society[6].

Last but not least, the interests of school administrators must be taken into account. As managers and custodians of these materials, they are in the unenviable position of having to decide whether to regard them as materials of historical interest and therefore worthy of protection and conservation, or as obsolete objects to be replaced. In this regard, the Decree of the Ministry of Education, University and Research no. 129 of 28 August 2018[7], at the art. 34 (*Sale of end-of-life materials and no longer usable goods*) states that:

> 1. [...] end-of-life, obsolete and no longer usable assets are discarded by the schools by order of the school manager, after determining their value, which is calculated on the basis of the inventory value less depreciation, i.e. on the basis of the second-hand value of similar assets, as determined by a specific internal committee.

The problem of disposing of obsolete school materials became extremely urgent during the recent period of the Covid-19 health emergency, which brought a sudden and not always positive acceleration for schools. Suddenly forced to look for new spaces that would guarantee the necessary social distance and, at the same time, to purchase new, more functional furniture for this purpose, schools

---

[6] Given the vast literature on this topic, I will limit myself to mentioning the Italian work by Bortolotti, Calidoni, Mascheroni, & Mattozzi (2008) and, for a summary vision, the collection of essays edited by Branchesi, Iacono, & Riggio (2019).

[7] See Decree no. 129 of 28 August 2018: *Regulation containing general instructions on the administrative and accounting management of educational institutions, pursuant to Article 1, paragraph 143, of Law no. 107 of 13 July 2015* (GU General Series no. 267 of 11-16-2018). The complete text is freely available online on the website of the Official Journal: <ttps://www.gazzettaufficiale.it/ atto/stampa/serie_generale/originario> (01.09.2022).

had to quickly discard materials and furniture (Pic. 4). Precisely in February 2021 the Ministry of Education took steps to organically regulate the procedures for eliminating assets from the inventory (inventory disposal) by issuing specific *Guidelines for the management of school heritage and inventories* that replaced the previous instructions (notes prot. no. 8910 of 2011 and no. 2233 of 2012)[8]. In the text, assets subject to elimination are classified and defined as follows:

– *End-of-life assets*: these include unusable, broken or damaged assets for which repair would be uneconomical;

– *Obsolete assets*: this category includes functioning assets that are outdated from a technological point of view and also in terms of the care of the public interest pursued;

– *Unusable assets*: these are assets which, although intact and capable of being reused, no longer meet the needs of the activity being carried out[9].

For end-of-life assets, the following procedures are laid down: public sale or, in the event of an unsuccessful tender, transfer against payment through negotiation or, then, the free transfer "to non-economic public bodies or, alternatively, to non-profit bodies (NPOs, associations for the promotion of local culture and tourism, parishes, social promotion bodies etc.)" and, finally, in the

---

[8]   See also Ministerial note 23.02.2021, prot. no. 4083.

[9]   The definitions are given in Par. 4.1.9. *Elimination of assets from the inventory* of the Ministerial note 23.02.2021, prot. no. 4083: *Guidelines for the management of assets and inventories of State educational and school establishments, pursuant to Article 29, par. 3, of Inter Ministerial Decree no. 129 of 28 August 2018: Regulation containing general instructions on the administrative and accounting management of educational institutions, pursuant to Article 1, paragraph 143, of Law no. 107 of 13 July 2015*, p. 28. For the sake of completeness, it should be recalled that the "assets subject to elimination" also include the "resulting materials", i.e. the materials left over "after processing or waste materials".

event of a negative outcome, the definitive dismantling (*ibid.*, pp. 28-29). For assets that are obsolete or unusable for school needs, consideration is given to sale by auction, or "by private negotiation to other non-economic public bodies" and, in the event of a nega-tive outcome, free transfer but "only to another school" and, as a last resort, landfill (*ibid.*, pp. 29-30).

Pic. 1.6. *(above, on the left) Obsolescence vs conservation. One of many images of old furniture that was discarded after the renovation of school equipment and the intro-duction of distance rules during the Covid-19 health emergency (photo from 2020, source: web);* **Pic. 1.7**. *(on the right) Reconstruction of a school classroom in the 1960s (source: Monopoli 2012).*

Pic. 1.8. *(on the right) A Vallardi anatomical bust (ca. 1950-1960) partially damaged but of great historical and scientific value, partially damaged but preserved at MUDESC – "Paolo e Ornella Ricca" Museum of the School History at the University of Macerata (photo by Marta Brunelli)*

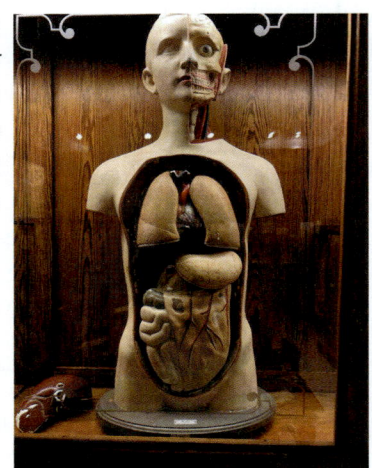

But where does the status of an "obsolete object" (Pic. 6) end and the status of a historical testimony and museum object begin? (Pic. 7). How can we be sure that an unusable object does not have a historical-documentary interest, which is not actual but at least potential – in the eyes of a specialist – because it is worn-out or outdated?

Finally, what are the criteria for determining that an "unusable, broken or damaged" asset has not already acquired such a historical-documentary value (Pic. 8) that its repair is not only convenient, but even advantageous from a scientific and cultural point of view?

Without compromising the scientific, educational and cultural need – and obligation – of schools to modernise their equipment and provide modern services tailored to the teaching and learning needs of today's world, one wonders if it is possible to rethink the logic of "disposal". For instance, it would be sufficient to incorporate all those museums, conservation institutes, research centres, universities and other stakeholders involved in the history of schooling and education into the processing chain for end-of-life school materials. This would potentially interest them in preserving some (or some samples) of the materials that would otherwise be destined for disposal. The themes identified by the SIPSE Committee and explored in more detail in this volume precisely reflect these issues (and the related criticalities) – of a historical-scientific, cultural and pedagogical nature – that have arisen in recent years around the historical school material. However, all the issues point to the fundamental difficulty posed by the lack of a clear legal framework for a potential new category of "school heritage"[10].

---

[10] The term "school and educational heritage" was first proposed by Monica Ferrari and her research group at the University of Pavia, where the Cen-

The questions from which this paper arises are mainly the following: do school historical materials have characteristics that make them worthy of protection and preservation for their cultural interest? Do they have a precise historical-documentary value because they are material testimonies of the evolution of pedagogical ideas, teaching practices and school culture of a nation? Finally, is it possible, based on this premise, to consider a conservation policy aimed at the protection of cultural values and interests which, if not current, are at least potential?

This essay, like the others in this volume, aims at shedding light on these peculiarities and on the intrinsic value of a heterogeneous complex of materials that a large Italian and international scientific community, animated by historians of school and education, pedagogists, but also children's literature scholars and historians of books and publishing, have unanimously recognised for almost twenty years under the definition of "historical-educational heritage". An increasingly mature and complex reflection on this heritage has been definitively consolidated, that is, a careful reflection not only on the most exquisite historiographical aspects, but also on the issues of its conservation and valorisation (Sani 2018 and 2019). Which is the focus of this book.

---

tre for Study and Valorisation of School and Educational Cultural Assets was founded in 2006 (dissolved in 2014). The Municipality of Mantua had entrusted to the same group one of the first projects for the collection and systematic description of the historical-educational materials in the city's public schools and later entitled *The Objects' Lessons*. Because of this experience, the definition of "school heritage" was presented by Ferrari in 2007 in a seminar on educational research and valorisation of school libraries and archives, which are fully covered by the legal definition of a cultural asset. On that occasion, interesting reflections were posed for the very first time on the composite nature of school heritage as well as on the problems related to its management. See Ferrari, Panizza, & Morandi (2008) and Ferrari & Morandi (2017).

The role of historical-educational research in heritage and musealisation processes of school material culture

The recent trends that have emerged over the last twenty years in historical-educational research have profoundly revolutionised the relationship between history and pedagogy at a methodological and epistemological level. Such development has helped to focus historians' interest on the value of the new sources represented by school materialities as crucial testimonies of educational practices and values[11].

From the history of pedagogy to the study of school materiality: Not just a lexical change

Until the 1960s the main historiographical reference models in Italy were still characterised by an idealistic and Gentile-like approach, according to which the only object of study was the *history of pedagogy*, identified with the history of pedagogical ideas and theories and the authors who expressed them. This vision had already shown the first signs of opening up to other research agendas in the 1950s and 1960s, with the emergence of new historiographies that paid more attention to the history of the school and the history of education. These were seen as the result of a dialectic between pedagogical models and broader socio-economic and political issues, such as illiteracy, schooling processes, and the world of work. This change took place, on the one hand, thanks to Marxist historiography and was expressed in the work by Dina Bertoni Jovine *Storia della scuola popolare in Italia* (History of the Mass

---

[11] In the vast bibliography on the topic I shall confine myself here to referring to the following theoretical works: Santoni Rugiu & Trebisacce (1983), Becchi (1987), Macchietti (1990), Ulivieri (2015), Zago (2015), Borruso (2019), De Fort (2002), Sani (2019 and 2011, pp. 8-14).

School in Italy), published in 1953. This book was, not surprisingly, republished in 1962 under the title *Storia dell'educazione popolare in Italia* (History of Mass Education in Italy). And it was precisely in the academic year 1964/1965 that the first Chair of *History of the school and educational institutions* was created in Padua, marking, in a way, the beginning of a new cultural and scientific season.

On the other hand, this shift was deeply influenced by the French historiography of the Annales, whose new investigations into everyday life, the history of mentalities, the long-term approach, the comparison of cultural models and the close exchange with the social sciences would have a strong impact. The Eighties were the years in which a new generation of scholars of the history of education began to work, gathering around the new Italian Research Centre for Educational History (CIRSE-Centro Italiano per la Ricerca Storico-Educativa), which was created in 1980. These scholars took up the challenge posed by new journals, such as *Studi di storia dell'educazione* by Fabrizio Ravaglioli (1980-1995), or innovative works such as the collection *Storia dell'educazione* edited by Egle Becchi (1987), and finally the criticism moved by scholars such as Marino Raicich, who at the beginning of the 1980s, denounced the lack of tools and methodologies used in Italian studies on the history of education and schools (Raicich 1982, pp. 19-23). These years therefore marked the beginning of a new era in which Italian historiography opened itself to new historiographical approaches and to an interdisciplinary debate, stimulated by an increasingly fruitful exchange with the international community.

School culture and school materiality as new historiographical paradigms

When in the 1990s the French historians Dominique Julia (1995a)[12] and André Chervel (1996 and 1998) introduced the first innovative reflections on *school culture*, all the research groups on history of education – first the Belgian (Depaepe & Simon 1995), Iberian (Viñao Frago 1998, Ruiz Berrio 2000, Escolano Benito 2005) and Anglo-Saxon historians (Grosvenor, Lawn, & Rousmaniere 1999) – also saw new lines of research opening up at the international level. The new historiographical approach had two main directions. First, it encouraged the study of the evolution of school subjects and teaching practices, within the framework of cultural history (Popkewitz, Franklin, & Pereyra 2001, Julia, Pazzaglia, Betti, & Tognon 2004, Belhoste, 2005). Second, it highlighted school material culture as a fertile field of study, offering a wide range of new sources. Historians of education had rarely considered these sources, except for a few pioneering reflections. As signalled by Mirella D'Ascenzo (1997, pp. 16-18), Dario Ragazzini (1997) had already identified the concept of the "material life of the school" intended as the school routine, arising from the interweaving of hours and norms, spaces and behaviours associated with the school. Although it has been noted that this concept did not directly refer to school materiality intended as a set of school material testimonies (Meda & Polenghi 2021, pp. 62-63), however it can be argued that the Ragazzini's dimension of school routine somehow anticipates Julia's definition of *school culture*. Indeed, the Italian historian refers to the school as a manifestation of activities that are daily and concretely shaped by the two dimensions

---

[12] The article had a wide international resonance, as evidenced by its almost immediate translation into Spanish (Julia 1995b) and Italian (Julia 1996).

of time (a true "material condition" of teaching) and space, which is "defined and traversed by affective, mental and social relations, with emotional dynamics, cognitive actions and rules of behaviours" (Ragazzini 1997, p. 5). Ragazzini continues:

> Introducing the problem of time means characterising a space and unravelling – in their institutional form – the relationship between teachers and learners, the interplay between content, methods, goals, and operating conditions, and the connection between social figures and ways of life. A "who, when and how?" that cannot be explained without combining all three answers; among the three aspects, the one that has remained most in the shadows so far is the one related to the 'when' (*ibid.*, p. 7).

Egle Becchi's position had also been critical of the "shadows" of historical-educational research at the time. In fact, in 1987, she had pointed out how all those minor and apparently "uninteresting" objects that are part of the so-called "school's *outillage*, equipment, teaching furniture of the classroom" represented by "desks, blackboards, books, different exercise books for each class, wall posters for alphabet, geography and science lessons, registers, pens, black and coloured pencils, uniforms that differ according to gender, school and class, colours or, rather, non-colours of the classroom walls" (Becchi 1987, p. 26), had remained in the gaps of the history of educational processes. Today, these passages sound very suggestive and premonitory of the direction that research would clearly have taken in Italy in a few years' time.

After the works of Julia and Chervel, and thanks to the fruitful exchanges with the Spanish historians of education who immediately welcomed and cultivated the new historiographical category of *school culture*, the same lines of investigation were adopted by the emerging historical-educational research groups in Italy. In fact, at the Catholic University of Milan Luciano Pazzaglia founded the journal *Annali di storia dell'educazione e delle istituzioni scolastiche* (1994-) in the 1990s; at the University of Turin Giorgio Chiosso initiated unprecedented inter-university research and projects that'll lead to the creation of fundamental repertoires of historical-educational sources (Chiosso 1989, 1992, 1993, 1997, 2000, 2003 and 2008; Chiosso & Sani 2013). This was the backdrop for the establishment by Roberto Sani of the Research Centre for the History of Textbooks and Children's Literature at the University of Macerata in 2004, which led to the creation of the international journal *History of Education & Children's Literature* in 2006, and the "Paolo e Ornella Ricca" Museum of School History in 2009.

As we can see, in the transition between the old and the new millennium, historical-educational research has renewed scientific approaches, tools and languages, which have led to the birth of a scientific production aimed at reconstructing the characteristics and evolution of everyday school life and its actors, times and spaces – represented in particular by the classroom – where this everyday life took place. From this point of view, the classroom becomes the fulcrum where the furniture and teaching aids are the traces that allow us to reconstruct educational activities, behaviours and practices: some of them hidden or forgotten in what has been defined as a real *black box of schooling* (Braster, Grosvenor, & del Pozo Andrés 2011).

Not immune to this *material turn* in educational historiography (Gaspar da Silva, Meda, & de Souza 2021; Meda & Polenghi 2021) has been the Italian scholarly community, which in recent years has given life to an increasingly interesting scientific production on almost all aspects of school materiality. To understand the importance of this research, it is worth mentioning the different materials object of investigation, starting with exercise books and diaries, with reference to the studies by Montino (2005), Meda (2006a, 2006b), Genovesi (2008), Meda, Montino, & Sani (2010), Sani (2013).

Other objects or research are the classroom (Pruneri 2006, pp. 116-123, Pruneri 2014, Spampani 2016) and its furniture (De Giorgi 2014, Meda 2016a, 2016b, Brunelli & Meda 2017, Di Biasio & Gargano 2021), as well as school architecture (Giorgi 2016, Marcarini 2016, Viola 2016, 2018a, 2018b and 2019). Studies have been published also on gymnastic aids by Elia (2012, 2016, 2017 and 2021) and Brunelli & Meda (2017), on museum-cabinets and teaching boxes (D'Ascenzo 2008, 2014 and 2020; (Pizzigoni 2015, 2020 and 2022a), teaching posters and wall maps (Cossetto 2009, Targhetta 2015, Meda 2022), teaching and pedagogical aids for nursery schools (Ferrari, Morandi, & Platé 2008 and 2011), or scientific aids (Brunelli 2018a, 2020 and 2023; Barausse, Andreassi, & Viola 2021). Other subjects of research are represented by school photographs (Giorgi 2011, Giorgi & Franchi 2012, Vanni 2015, Brunelli 2014, 2016 and 2017b), light projections, teaching film strips and other audiovisual aids for educational use (De Berti 2004, Lombardi, 2010, Mazzei & Alovisio 2016, Alovisio 2018, Callegari 2020, Targhetta 2020 and 2022).

The role of scientific associations at the international level

Thanks to this development of research, the historical-educational heritage has become not only the catalyst of specialised studies, but also the fulcrum of heritagisation and musealisation processes that have spread in different ways and historical stages in European and non-European countries.

Since the 2000s, a strong impulse has come from scientific associations specifically dedicated to the historical-educational heritage and created by communities of educational historians oriented towards the new historiographical paradigm of school culture. Historians have also had the merit of setting up new associations to promote not only research, but also the valorisation of school collections and the creation of museums, both in local areas and in universities. The Portuguese and Spanish cases are emblematic: in Portugal, on the occasion of the *I Foro Ibérico de Museísmo Pedagógico* organised in 2001 by the newly created MUPEGA (Museo Pedagógico de Galicia), RIHMIE-*Rede de Investigadores em História e Museologia da Infância e da Educação* was born in 2001, and in Spain, SEPHE-*Sociedad Española para el Estudio del Patrimonio Histórico Educativo*, was founded in 2004 as an autonomous unit of SEDHE (*Sociedad Española de Historia de la Educación*). Thanks to these scientific communities, a series of national and international meetings have been promoted, scientific journals have been published (such as the SEPHE's *Boletín informativo*, to which the journal *Cabás* was added in 2009, dedicated exclusively to the historical-educational heritage (Hernández Huerta, Payà Rico, & Grau Vidal 2021), and new lines of research and valorisation for the educational heritage have been dictated.

This important associative activity has also catalysed the creation of new associations at international level, as well as the renewal of of other already existing ones. For example, the new *Red Iberoamericana para la Investigación y Difusión del Patrimonio Histórico-Educativo* (RIDPHE) was created in 2008 by the University of Campinas (in the State of São Paulo, Brazil). The aim is to bring together educational historians from all over South America to promote historical research on school collections in Latin American realities and to pedagogically valorise school collections and archives. On the other hand, the *Association des Amis du Musée National de l'Education*, founded by Serge Chassagne on the occasion of the opening of the National Museum of Education in Rouen in 1983, was an existing reality. Active until the end of 1990s, it was relaunched in 2012 by opening its membership to students, teachers, researchers, families and citizens; then, in 2017, AMNEPE (*Amis du Musée national de l'Education, des musées de l'école et du patrimoine éducatif*) was born, bringing together one hundred and seventy museums of educational heritage (Mieussens & Bouhier 2017). In the wake of this associative movement, the Italian SIPSE (*Società Italiana del Patrimonio Storico-Educativo*) was born, which now cooperates with its counterparts in other countries and continents, although it was founded only in 2017 (Brunelli 2017a). Since 2018, SIPSE has organised a biennial national conference with the participation of foreign colleagues, published dedicated series and promoted the activities of four committees analysing different aspects of school heritage: from archives to museums, libraries and, of course, the cataloguing of school materials.

As a result of the mentioned associations' activities and the advancement of research, the educational heritage is now perceived as a segment of cultural heritage that is widely recognized throughout the world. This is confirmed by the definitive consolidation in many languages, since the beginning of 2000, of the concept and term *educational heritage* and its homologues: *patrimonio histórico-educativo* in Spanish-speaking countries, *patrimônio histórico-educacional* in Portuguese and Brazilian contexts, and *patrimoine éduca-*

tif (or *patrimoine pédagogique*) in French-speaking areas. Over the last twenty years, this term has come to denote a very specific category of heritage – both tangible and intangible[13] – which is accepted not only by people working in the world of education (historians or theorists of education, teachers, or heritage educators), but also by museum professionals, heritage specialists and historians in various fields (book history, social history etc.). In this respect, it is also worth noting that in the last two decades *educational heritage* has become the subject of interdisciplinary research especially aimed at recovering the traces of a cultural and national identity. This is the case in India, where the tangible and intangible traces of a thousand-year-old educational tradition are being studied as a process of decolonisation (Singh 2017 and 2022). Or in Kazakhstan, where the creation of the MHKES-Museum of the History of Kazakhstan Education System (Ibrayeva, Kalkeyeva, Khamitovna, & Sanakulova 2015) is seen as part of the process of building and consolidating the cultural identity of the nation.

Categories and subcategories of a "new" heritage: From historical-educational heritage to school historical heritage

The development of research, the increasing attention paid to the material culture of schools and the emergence of scientific asso-

---

[13] Intangible educational heritage is made up of teaching practices used in the classroom, as well as nursery rhymes, proverbs, sayings, customs, and behaviours linked to specific moments of school life, festivals, songs and celebrations. Many of these traces are passed through oral memories, which can be found in autobiographies as well as in oral sources. Intrinsically linked to the tangible testimonies, the intangible heritage is its fundamental complement and its historiographical and hermeneutic enrichment in many ways. See Yanes Cabrera (2007, 2008 and 2010) and Viñao Frago (2012).

ciations dedicated to the conservation and valorisation of the educational heritage have led to an increasing musealisation of the objects considered to be part of this heritage. The creation of museums, large or small, is becoming more and more frequent and is being carried out at different levels by different players: from schools as a way of recovering their own history and tradition, to private individuals, cultural associations and local authorities wishing to revitalise their areas culturally and touristically. This phenomenon is constantly expanding and now sees the inauguration of new realities every year[14]. As a result of these processes, the concept of historical-educational heritage has now gained recognition within the scientific community as a genuine interpretive category. On the one hand, it can guide new lines of research based on the study of ever-new material sources, integrating traditional sources (Meda 2019). On the other hand, it has established itself as a new category of heritage that is now widely accepted, even beyond academic circles and within civil society, in a common, broad, and inclusive definition, i.e. that encompasses a wide range of objects and materials that need to be preserved and communicated (Sani 2019).

But what are the objects that are part of this heritage?

---

[14] Consider that the most recent museum included in the database of OPeN-MuSE Observatory of Macerata at the moment in which we are writing, is represented by *Siror School Museum*, which was created with a project of the two former teachers Flavio Taufer and Piero Depaoli in 2019, activated in November 2021 and officially inaugurated at the old primary school in Siror on May 26th, 2022. The museum is part of the *Small Museums in Primiero*, a network established for the valorisation of local cultural heritage in the Municipality of Primiero San Martino di Castrozza (TN). See the museum sheet in OPeNMuSE: <https://www.unimc.it/cescom/it/openmuse> (11.12.2022); the website of the network *Piccoli Musei a Primiero* is <https://piccolimuseiaprimiero.it/> (11.12.2022).

In this respect, it is necessary to make a first distinction in order to better clarify the meaning of the two terms *educational heritage* and *school heritage*, which are often used as if they were interchangeable. However, they represent the same difference that exists between education and school, and therefore between the history of education and the history of the school.

The history of education reconstructs the evolution of all the methods and forms in which education, understood as "a continuous process of transmitting the culture of the adult generations to the younger generations" (Santamaita 2013, p. 6), has materialised throughout human history. This transmission process takes place in different contexts, which are not limited to the school world but are extended to include many other realities in a perspective of lifelong learning. The history of education is thus concerned with the reconstruction of educational processes that have developed in the past within all the educational agencies – from the family to the school and beyond i.e. through religious institutions, youth or sports associations, political parties or trade unions, in the workplace and in other educational settings – covering the universe of education in its formal, non-formal and informal tripartite division.

Instead, the history of the school focuses on the historical development of only one of the educational institutions listed above: the school as a structured, public and mass institution, and a direct emanation of the modern state. Indeed, with the emergence of national states in the 19th century, schools were given the task of educating the people of the nation, promoting the national language and creating a sense of common belonging. The characteristics of laicity, compulsory attendance, free of charge and universality make the modern school one of the most important educational institutions, whose funding, territorial organisation and internal regulation are managed by the central state through a specific legislation, ministry and state representatives.

Given these premises, it is evident that the historical-educational heritage is a vast category of material, comprising testimonies from various educational contexts (family, school, professional, leisure, political, associative, sports and so on) where individuals engage in learning throughout their lives. On the other hand, the school heritage is a subset of the previous one, or rather, it is encompassed within it, yet distinct. In fact, it comprises only the traces of the history of schooling, organised by the States to provide education exclusively imparted in public schools and regulated by dedicated laws.

To better illustrate the two concepts, here is a chart (Pic. 1.9) that clearly shows:

1) the most limited dimension of school history, as compared to the history of education;

2) consequently, the most limited dimension of the school heritage (compared to the educational one, which encompasses it). In other words, while it is true that the educational heritage includes the school heritage, the latter *does not coincide* with the former, but rather constitutes a distinct and identifiable component of it.

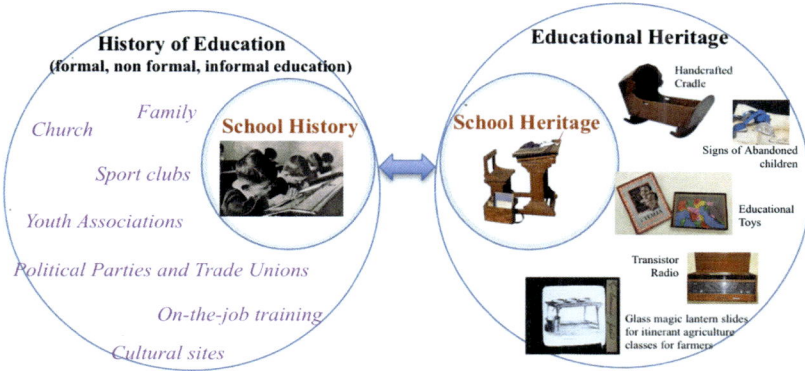

Pic. 1.9. *History of School as a subset of History of (formal, non-formal and informal) Education and school historical heritage as a subset of historical-educational heritage*

Given the vastness of educational heritage, it is not uncommon to find it in museums that are not specifically dedicated to education. The educational heritage can be preserved, for instance, in children's or toy museums, whose collections aim to narrate the history and culture of childhood through tangible traces related to all aspects of child-rearing. This includes baby care accessories (e.g. cradles or baby walkers, Pic. 1.10), children's clothing or furniture, and finally toys (Pic. 1.11), which are considered as true tools of enculturation (Neri 1977; Gianini Belotti 1973, pp. 87-102; Farnè 1998).

For the same reasons, educational heritage can also be seen in demo-ethno-anthropological museums, which often preserve materials related to family education and the upbringing of children as expressions of popular and local culture (Pics. 1.10-11). A particular educational (but not school) heritage is that preserved in the museums that reconstruct the history of ancient orphanages: the *Martinitt and Stelline* Institutes in Milan, founded in Milan in the 16th century, or the *Spedale degl'Innocenti* Florence, established in the 15th century. In the latter, for example, you can see the *segnali dei gettatelli* (the abandoned children's marks), i.e. the halved objects that mothers placed on their abandoned children in the hope of recognising them in the future (Pic. 1.12).

Pic. 1.10 *(on the left) Baby walker from the first half of the 20th century, Ostana Ethnographic Museum, CN (source: <https://libroaperto.comune.ostana.cn.it/ museo-etnografico-di-ostana>)*

Pic. 1.11 *(on the right) Toy Museum for children, Florence-Santo Stefano Lodigiano (LO) (source: <https://www.museodelgiocattolo.it/>)*

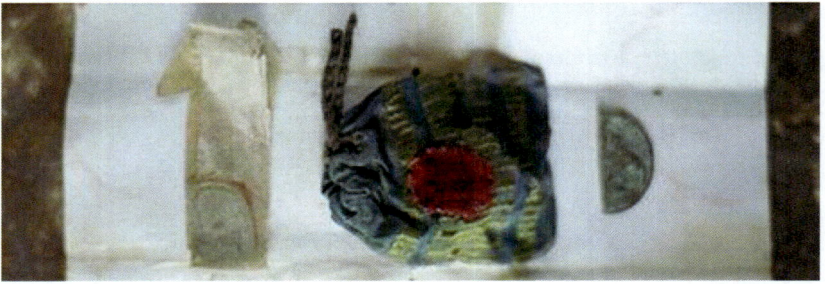

Pic. 1.12 *The gettatelli's marks: a piece of cloth, a fabric bag, half a brass medal (photo by G. Cozzi, source: Archive at Istituto degli Innocenti: <https://www.archivio.istitutodeglinnocenti.it/>)*

Another example is the objects that testify to the history of adult education, which largely takes place outside the formal education system. As a result, these material testimonies fall within the definition of educational heritage, rather than school heritage. This is the case of the materials of the *Radio Elettra School*, founded in Turin in 1951, which was the first to offer correspondence courses for the training of technicians in the electrical and telecommunications sector, a key industry in post-war Italy (Pics. 1.13a-b).

Pic. 1.13*a. Collection of the periodic handouts from the course Tube Stereo Radio. Ph. D. Fornasiero (source: <https://www.historybit.it/scuola-radio-elettra/>, 03.04.2025)*

Pic. 1.13*b. A Model 865 tube stereo radio, which the learners had to assemble at the end of the course. Years 1950s-60s. Ph. D. Fornasiero (source: <https://www.history-bit.it/scuola-radio-elettra/>, 03.04.2025)*

After these examples, it will be easier to understand the differences between the educational and the school heritage. In particular, the latter – which is the subject of this book – has its own specific characteristics compared to the former. And it is these particularities that make it difficult to assimilate it to other types of heritage, as will be explained in the following paragraph.

Specificity and composition of the school heritage

We have seen that the historical-educational heritage is very broad and difficult to outline, as it potentially includes all the evidence of the history of education considered in its three formal (school), non-formal and informal dimensions. Rather, school heritage is "evidence of the forms and methods by which schooling has been achieved in time and space" (Jalla, Lonjon, Pizzigoni, & Vuillet 2011, p. 53). In short, it is a testimony to the evolution of state school education.

The category of school heritage is also internationally recognised, as is shown by the clear acceptance and adoption of similar terms in other languages: *Patrimonio histórico-escolar*, *Patrimoine scolaire* or *School heritage*. Regarding the quantity and type of materials that make up this heritage, it must be said that a detailed classification has been consolidated particularly in the Italian literature of the last decade (Meda 2010, pp. 490-491 and 2013, pp. 171-172, 195-197)[15]. Based on this research, we can list the various components of the school heritage as follows:

- *School libraries*;

- *School archives*;

---

[15] Other interesting taxonomies have been proposed by the Education Museum at the University of Padua (see the web page *Collezioni*, <https://www.fisppa.unipd.it/servizi/museo-educazione/collezioni> [12.09.2022]), and by Jalla, Lonjon, Pizzigoni, & Vuillet (2011, pp. 49-53).

– *School furniture*, i.e. all the furniture that makes schools functional for the institutional mission, such as black-boards, school desks and chairs, teachers' desks with the associated platforms. All of these pieces of furniture were prescribed by law and, in the case of desks, reflected precise hygienic, health, as well as pedagogical require-ments. (Meda 2016b, pp. 52-62);

– *The furnishings of the school* are all those minor materials that, at first sight, seem to be of little importance, but in fact are significant additions to the classroom, such as the portraits of the authorities, and the crucifix, which were also required by law. To these can be added flags, framed titles, diplomas or awards, framed historical pho-tographs, framed photographs of graduates, punishment tools, the brazier or the stove, the small class library, the clothes hooks, shelves for school maps, school bells, teaching boxes for specimens, etc.;

– *Disciplinary teaching aids*, i.e. all the tools and equipment used by the teacher to support the teaching of each sub-ject. Teaching aids for literacy (primers, wall-mounted or mobile alphabets, nomenclature posters, etc.), history (wall charts, synoptic tables, etc.), geography (globes and planispheres, planetariums, geographical maps, models, world maps, etc.), arithmetic (abacuses and other calcula-tion tools, number rods, measures of capacity and weight, geometric models, squares and rulers, Pythagorean ta-bles, etc.), natural sciences (plastic models, stuffed ani-mals, minerals and fossils collections, herbariums, wall charts of anatomy, zoology, botany, etc.), music (musical instruments, tuning forks, metronomes, etc.), physical ed-

ucation (gym equipment), product samples (school museums as sample boxes of materials for object lessons);

- *Pedagogical aids* – defined by the Museum of the University of Padua as "aids of authorship"[16] i.e. teaching aids
  that are not focused on a particular subject, but are transversal to all the school subjects, since they have been created by pedagogists within the framework of their own
  specific teaching methods (such as the teaching materials
  designed by Froebel, Montessori, Agazzi, Freinet, etc.);

- *Educational games*: teaching kits that also teach through
  games at school, as shown by catalogues of school materials with (industrial or handicraft) building block games,
  flashcards, educational puzzles, which have been applied
  from time to time to various subjects, from mathematics
  to geography, literacy etc. (Pics. 1.14-15);

- *Multimedia aids*: technological tools to support disciplinary teaching, ranging from magic lanterns to film
  projectors, radios, record players, portable cassette players, overhead projectors, slide projectors, etc.;

- *Teaching aids created by teachers* in imitation or anticipation
  of industrial materials (drawings, geographical maps,
  mathematical aids, etc.);

- *Stationery*: inks, pens and nibs, pencil cases, bookmarks,
  portable inkpots;

- *Pupils' and/or teachers' kit*: bows, school aprons, school

---

[16] See the webpage *Collezioni* of the Education Museum at the University of
Padua,   <https://www.fisppa.unipd.it/servizi/museo-educazione/collezi-
oni> (10.07.2022).

uniforms, school bags, lunch boxes, brooches, or badges;

– *Exercise books and diaries*: exercise books containing pupils' works and drawings, but also teachers' school diaries or exercise books, etc.;

– *School architecture*, i.e., all the historic buildings that have been created or have been used as schools (Meda 2019). This heritage – the so-called *built heritage of schools*[17] – includes a whole series of other different elements, which are associated with schools, such as wall decorations (frescoes, mosaics, majolica, etc.) and wall inscriptions (such as plaques and commemorative tablets for the history of the school or for school personalities). For the latter ones, the scientific community has recently coined the new category of "public school memories"[55]. Other elements and structures outside the school buildings are also of particular interest: school courtyards and gardens with associated furniture, botanical gardens or even adjacent squares and streets;

– *Works of art*: these are the works of art (drawings, paintings, sculptures, etc.), kept in schools, including those made by pupils or alumni, teachers, artists, etc.

---

[17] The educational valorisation of the school built heritage was the focus of the European Erasmus+ project "Identity & Innovation" (2021-2022), which was led by the Heilig Hartinstituut Pedagogische Humaniora (BE). The «Paolo e Ornella Ricca» School Museum at the University of Macerata took part in the project through the figures of Marta Brunelli (Principal Investigator of the project) and Fabio Targhetta (Director of the Museum and member of the local research unit).

Pic. 1.14. *Wooden building block games, circa 1900-1940.*

MUDESC-Museo della Scuola «Paolo e Ornella Ricca», University of Macerata (photos by Marta Brunelli)

Pic. 1.15 *The geopuzzle Comporre l'Italia: giuoco geotarsico-istruisce divertendo (Putting together Italy: geographic puzzle which educates through play), 1939-1943.*

MUDESC-Museo della Scuola «Paolo e Ornella Ricca», University of Macerata (photos by Marta Brunelli)

As we can see from the above list, recent historical-educational research has focused on the study of an increasingly wide and heterogeneous range of objects, destined, moreover, to expand as research progresses. Despite this heterogeneity, however, all these objects share an intrinsic characteristic that makes them coherent with each other: they are part of a true *universality of assets*. I have already used this term (Brunelli 2013), borrowing it from other disciplinary fields. From the juridical language, on the one hand, where the concept of "universality of movable assets" refers to a plurality of things belonging to a single person or having "a unitary destination", such as the books of a library or the paintings in a picture gallery (Art. 816 of the Civil Code). And, above all, from the archival theory, on the other hand. In fact, in 1937, Giorgio Cencetti described the archive as a universality, i.e. a *universitas rerum* whose unity is based on the fact that each of its components "from the very beginning has carried within itself the constraint of a common destination, which is summed up in fulfilling the functions of the body or of the person" that created the archive (Cencetti 1937, p. 8).

Unlike the educational objects, historical school objects come from the same source (public schools). They have therefore been conceived, produced (by hand or industrially) and finally used for the same and sole purpose: to fulfil the institutional mission of the school, which is to educate the citizens of a nation. On the one hand, this common purpose makes them all coherent and inseparable from each other. On the other hand, it makes them – individually and collectively – testimonies of Italian school history as a public institution and an emanation of the national State. A history

that is therefore a fundamental part of the history of every nation
and an essential element of national identity.

What protection for what heritage? Critical issues and proposals for the legal recognition of "school heritage"

The previous pages have shown on the one hand the richness and
the heterogeneity of school heritage and, on the other hand the
stratification of meanings and values (historical, cultural, pedagogical, social, identity and scientific) that have already been
invested in this heritage, not only by scholars and researchers, but
also by teachers and headmasters and, last but not least, by pupils,
families and communities. However, this heritage is in constant
danger of being damaged or dispersed. This is particularly true
where there is a lack of awareness of the historical value (actual
or potential) of these materials, which are kept in warehouses and
sheds, often poorly stored, awaiting transfer or final disposal. This
situation makes us wonder what kind of legal protection can be
given to school heritage.

A first hypothesis, already considered together with the experts,
would include the school's assets under the umbrella of "cultural
heritage", as defined in the art. 2, 10 and 11 of the Code of Cultural
Heritage and Landscape (Legislative Decree no. 42/2004). However,
this hypothesis – while suggestive and certainly inspired by the
objective lack of any form of protection and conservation of school
assets – runs into some critical issues.

On closer examination, the very diversity and heterogeneity
of school historical objects – which is certainly an essential and
distinctive feature of this heritage – could at the same time be an

obstacle to the concrete identification of the objects to be protected for the purposes of a legal definition.

The multidisciplinary nature of school heritage is its *typical feature*, which distinguishes it from similar materials collected in other museums[18]. However, this same feature risks making it difficult to distinguish which objects require a protection code from those that do not.

On the other hand, the recognition of a new legal notion of "school heritage" runs up against the fact that it includes categories of objects that are already recognised as cultural heritage under the Code. Examples are: geographical maps, historical photographs, audiovisual supports, but also memorial stones, inscriptions, frescoes or other valuable wall decorations and scientific collections. Thus, the legislator has already selected cultural assets on the basis of a relevant cultural interest and in compliance with the above-mentioned principle of *typicality* that distinguishes cultural objects.

As it is known, in fact, with regard to the assets that are publicly owned, Art. 10 of the Code (*Cultural Assets*) identifies the following cultural assets: "archives and single documents" of public bodies and institutions (subparagraph 2, letter b); state and public "book collections in libraries" (*ibid.*, letter c); rare and valuable manuscripts, autographs, correspondence, incunabula, as well as books, prints and engravings with related matrices (subparagraph 4, letter c); "rare and valuable" geographical maps and musical scores (*ibid.*, letter d); "rare and valuable" photographs "with related negatives and matrices", cinematographic films and audiovisual media in general (*ibid.*, letter e); "artistic or historic" parks and gardens (*ibid.*, letter f).

Other types, which are covered by Art. 11 (*Assets subject to special protection provisions*), are added to these assets and listed as follows: "frescoes, coats of arms, graffiti, memorial stones, inscriptions, tabernacles and other ornaments on buildings, whether or not exposed to public view" (subparagraph 1, letter a); "paintings, sculptures, graphic works and other works of art, created by a living author or whose execution is less than seventy years old" (*ibid.*, subparagraph d); "contemporary architecture of particular artistic merit" (*ibid.*, letter e); "photographs and related negatives and matrices, models of cinematographic or audiovisual works or sequences of moving images, documentation of sound or spoken demonstrations, production of which is more than twenty-five years old" (*ibid.*, letter f); "objects and instruments of interest for the history of science and technology, more than fifty years old» (*ibid.*, letter h).

There is therefore a risk of superimposing a new category of "school heritage" on existing ones, with obvious repercussions for the effectiveness and rationality of the related protection regime as well as organisational and economic sustainability.

Although one of the three essential characteristics of cultural assets (Sciullo 2020, pp. 40-41) – along with typicality and materiality – is the plurality of its categories, it is precisely the extreme diversity of school objects that may make it objectively difficult to include them in the legal concept of "cultural heritage"[18] in the technical-legal sense[19].

---

[18] With reference to the notion of cultural assets, please see Bartolini (2019) and Casini (2014).

[19] The Italian legislation on cultural assets, i.e. the *Code of Cultural Assets and Landscape* (Legislative Decree no. 42/2004), as well as the previous *Consolidated Law on cultural and environmental heritage provisions* (Legislative Decree no. 490/1999) attributes a precise meaning to the term *asset* compared

On the other hand, it is true that there is a tendency to broaden the definition of cultural heritage so that it can potentially include objects other than cultural assets.

This phenomenon is well known and has concerned firstly the recognition of an autonomous cultural value for landscape[20] as an object to be protected, distinct from landscape assets; and then, it has concerned the intangible cultural heritage, such as traditions and popular festivals[21]. In both cases, the phenomenon has been triggered by a growing pressure from the international legal system on these issues, as can be clearly seen in the European Landscape Convention of 2020 (Cartei 2007) and in the UNESCO Conventions of 2003 (*Convention for the Safeguarding of the Intangible Cultural Heritage*) and 2005 (*Convention for the Protection and the Promotion of the Diversity of Cultural Expressions*).

---

to the term *thing*. If the «thing» is the material object bearing a possible cultural interest, the «asset» is exclusively the object in which a specific value and cultural interest have been already explicitly identified by law, that is, such interest has been notified through a specific declaration by the competent territorial Superintendence. Regarding the kinds of «assets», which have been identified by law, see the next paragraph. Regarding the Italian legislation, see Tarasco (2004, p. 33).

[20] See the European Landscape Convention. See also Predieri (1969) (now republished in the journal «Il Capitale Culturale. Studies on the Value of Cultural Heritage», 9, 2014, <https://riviste.unimc.it/index.php/cap-cult/article/view/818>, 11.12.2022). and Civitarese Matteucci (2007).

[21] The notion of intangible cultural heritage, which was developed at an international level within the law on intangible cultural assets, identifies testimonies with a civilizational value, which are not included and represented in a *thing*, such as oral traditions, popular demonstrations, traditional knowledge, fairy tales, proverbs, etc. (Scovazzi, Ubertazzi, & Zagato, 2012). Well-known examples are the Sicilian Puppet Theatre, the Mediterranean diet, the Sardinian tenor singing and so on. See <https://www.unesco.it/it/italianellunesco/detail/189> (10.12.2022).

On the other hand, as appropriately underlined, the implications linked to the progressive broadening of the concept of cultural assets (Casini 2017, p. 11), or rather to the progressive affirmation of a plurality of cultural assets (Casini 2012), do not affect the notion of cultural assets and heritage, which has been typified by the Cultural Heritage and Landscape Code (Arts. 2, 10, 11). On the contrary, they confirm a plurality of concepts defined by different systems that outline a series of concentric circles[22], where the largest circle would represent cultural heritage as a product of culture in the anthropological sense. Within it, the smaller circle coincides with the notion of cultural asset used by the national legislator (and therefore provided for by the Code).

In short, the result would be a system of "parallel protections": a national protection for cultural assets intended in strict meaning, along with a "light" protection, based mainly on international conventions approved by UNESCO, and on measures implemented by Community institutions (Vitale 2010, p. 176).

The Council of Europe Framework Convention on the Value of Cultural Heritage for Society, signed in Faro on 27 October 2005 and ratified by Italy with Law no. 133 of 20 October 2020, is fully included in this trend (Cammelli 2020, Gualdani 2020, Carpentieri 2021).

As is well known, the new concepts of "cultural heritage" and "heritage community" were defined for the first time in the Faro Convention.

Art. 2, a, defines cultural heritage as "a group of resources inherited from the past which people identify, independently of owner-

---

[22] The image of concentric circles is also used by the doctrine to reposition the functions of the Ministry of Culture. See Covatta 2012, p. 24.

ship, as a reflection and expression of their constantly evolving values, beliefs, knowledge, and traditions. It includes all aspects of the environment resulting from the interaction between people and places through time". In Art. 2, b, the Convention defines "a heritage community" as consisting of people who value specific aspects of cultural heritage which they wish, within the framework of public action, to sustain and transmit to future generations".

The Convention is therefore based on an atypical notion of cultural heritage, since it is defined by bottom-up processes triggered off by heritage communities in the opposite direction to the qualification carried out by the legislator regarding *typical* cultural assets. This cultural heritage is defined as a result of a "reticular and centrifugal" movement, according to which the safeguarding is essentially the responsibility of the communities that support its relevance and merit, through a phenomenon like that observed for the so-called minor cultural assets, which are governed by regional and local regulations, such as historic sites (Cammelli 2017).

Therefore, the coexistence of different concepts, which are also defined on the basis of the disciplinary field (protection, valorisation, circulation), requires a greater flexibility in the identification of the *different* protection tools, also considering the different categories of assets that can be classified as cultural heritage, the characteristics and the state of the assets to be protected and the main needs to be satisfied.

From another perspective, it may be useful to remember that demo-ethno-anthropological heritage also falls within the Code's definition. We might then wonder whether school heritage is not a *species* of demo-ethno-anthropological heritage *genus*. In some cases, there is a close connection between the two types of heritage. For example, the old museumised Beckwith schools of the Waldensian communities in Piedmont have an ethnographic value since they reflect, at least in their origin, a very specific didactic model closely linked to the cultural and religious identity of these communities (Pizzigoni 2019). On the other hand, the school heritage in general (represented by the macro-sets of buildings, furniture, teaching aids, etc.) seems to be very different from the demo-ethno-anthropological heritage. While the latter is the expression of the practices, traditions and knowledge of a culture at a given historical moment, the former reflects the evolution of the national school system and is created and organised because of precise regulations issued by the State[23].

---

[23] To cite just one example, the regulation implementing the Casati Law had already prescribed the minimum equipment for classrooms in the first years of primary school, both in terms of furniture and essential teaching aids. In *Article 140* and 141 we can read that: "Without doubt, every school must be equipped with the following objects: 1. desks with a sufficient number of seats for all the pupils; 2. A teacher's desk with a lockable drawer and a small chair; 3. A lockable cupboard for storing books, writings, etc.; 4. a stove for heating the room; 5. the municipality must provide firewood for the winter season; […] 6. a picture representing the basic units and the real measures of the metric-decimal system; 7. a crucifix; 8. The portrait of the King. *Article 141*. In addition to these objects, the first class must have: 1. posters for teaching reading in accordance with the spelling book used by the pupils; 2. an abacus. *Art 142*. The upper secondary classes must have: 1. a terrestrial globe; 2. maps for the teaching of geography, in particular a world map and maps of Europe and Italy; 3. tables representing objects belonging to the first elements of the natural sciences; 4. relief models of the main geometric solids" (*Primary School Regulation of 15 September 1860*, approved as Royal Decree no. 4336 of 15 September 1860, a regulation implementing the Casati Law with attached primary school programmes).

In conclusion, one hypothesis

Despite the critical issues that seem to prevent historical school materials from being recognised as cultural assets under Art. 10 of the Code, it is possible to try to propose some alternative hypotheses.

As we have seen, for some time now there has been a progressive broadening of the notion of cultural heritage, which refers to some international conventions, the most recent of which is the Faro Convention. As a result, responsibility for protecting and valorising cultural heritage has extended beyond public institutions, reaching communities of citizens and, in particular, the *non-profit* sector. It is true that in many respects it is possible to see the need to update and rethink a concept of cultural heritage capable of guaranteeing the protection of what has an established and shared cultural value, such as the cultural heritage of schools. However, the way forward does not lie in overturning the Code's definition of cultural assets. In fact, the rigidity and restrictive approach of that system of protection, as well as its reliance on the regulatory and administrative competence of the State, may not be the most appropriate except in certain specific contexts, such as those envisaged by the Code.

In other words, the recognition of the cultural value of school heritage could find more effective tools of protection "outside the Code".

The same is known to happen with intangible heritage. Although it is recognised as culturally relevant, it is protected by the Code only if the requirement of materiality is met (see Art. 7 *bis* of the Code). Beyond the hypotheses of Art. 7 *bis*, intangible cultural heritage can be protected by other means, such as those provided by the local legal systems in terms of economic support, valorisation and conservation.

In conclusion, it seems interesting to briefly mention two international experiences that seem exemplary for a comparison with the Italian situation.

For example, in 2014, the Department of Education, Culture and Sport of the Autonomous Community of Cantabria, Spain – which is the only case in the European panorama – established the obligation for schools to preserve and valorise their heritage, which consists of "graphic, visual or audio documents, periodical publications, books, furniture, tools, teaching materials and other assets. These are not only the original heritage of each school, but also an important part of the heritage and history of education in Cantabria" (Gobierno de Cantabria 2014)[24]. In this case, however, the schools are not left to their own devices but are supported by the regional administration in the work of preserving, cataloguing, communicating and valorising their heritage, through a specialised research centre, the *Centro de Recursos, interpretación y Estudios en materia educativa* (CRIEME) in Polanco, created in 2005 by the Government of Cantabria[25].

In France, the prevailing attitude towards the preservation of school heritage was illustrated by two recent parliamentary questions asking the Ministry of Culture to intervene with specific instruments to safeguard the heritage of French primary and

---

[24] We would like to thank Luis M.ᵃ Naya Garmendia, Professor of Theory and History of Education at the University of the Basque Country, for sharing this information with Marta Brunelli on the occasion of the international conference *The School and Its Many Pasts* (Macerata, 12-15 December 2022).

[25] See Gobierno de Cantabria (2005) in the institutional website of CRIEME: <http://www.muesca.es/> (20.12.2022).

secondary schools (both in metropolitan France and overseas), and of normal schools with an ancient historical tradition. The Ministry – while reiterating that the responsibility for the management of these assets lies with the public body responsible for these schools – has highlighted that several subjects are already invested with the task of supporting schools with specific initiatives of census, cataloguing and conservation. The list of these subjects includes: the departmental archives services; the *Services Régionaux de l'Inventaire*; the museums already dedicated to the historical-educational heritage and supported by the Ministry of Culture (such as the *National Education Museum* in Rouen and the *Rural School Museum in Brittany*, Trégarvan); and, the services of the Ministry of Culture which support the valorisation of this heritage through conferences, study days, publications, exhibitions and workshops (Sénat Française 2019). Finally, the Ministry has added local initiatives for the census, conservation, and promotion of this school heritage, culminating in important projects to digitise school collections (Assemblée Nationale 2019). It is interesting to note, on the one hand, the emphasis on the "multi-institutional" nature of the management of this heritage and, on the other hand, the reference to the State concession as the "first measure of regulatory protection of this heritage", while the provisions on the heritage protection are considered as the second measure. In this way, a constellation of different subjects is configured to support the valorisation of this specific heritage with the tools already available.

In this sense, the suggestion made at the beginning of this essay can be considered a viable hypothesis, namely, to modify the procedures for dismantling and disposing of school materials by including other subjects among the possible recipients: public or private museums, cultural associations, academic and non-aca-

demic research centres interested in preserving school materials
and so on. This solution would not oblige schools to keep materials
(e.g. a lot of bulky furniture) that can no longer be used for normal
teaching, nor to house them in rooms to be specifically allocated
for this purpose. On the other hand, this proposal would create a
desirable support network for the conservation and valorisation of
these materials.

In short, we need to identify alternative means of protection to
those provided by the Code and to extend the responsibilities
involved beyond the public sphere, i.e. involving citizens, the
nonprofit sector and so on. This would make it possible to define
a protection system for cultural heritage that is open, flexible and,
above all, capable of responding to the needs expressed from time
to time by the communities of reference. In this way, it would be
possible to reduce the obligation for schools to directly manage
(and preserve) their heritage, in favour of a competence limited
to the coordination and monitoring of initiatives and activities
carried out by other subjects. Lastly, extending the responsibility
for safeguarding school heritage beyond the public sphere would
also make it possible to create a virtuous circle of cooperation
between the school and the territory, and between the local and
national dimensions.

Chapter 2

How to Catalogue a School Object?
Reflections and First Results[26]

Mara Orlando and Valeria Viola

Preface

The aim of the following pages is to present the first results of the Committee's work as a broader reflection which, on the one hand, examines the issue of cataloguing school materials in the context of research into the historical-educational heritage[27]. On the other hand, the issue is analysed in relation to the national cataloguing system managed by the Central Institute for Cataloguing and Documentation (Istituto Centrale per il Catalogo e la Documentazione, from now on ICCD), since this institute has not yet provided a descriptive card dedicated to school heritage, unlike

---

[26] This essay is the result of the joint work by Valeria Viola and Mara Orlando who, respectively, wrote paragraph 1. *Preface*, and paragraph 2. *Comparative analysis of the cataloguing cards existing today and recognized by ICCD referring to those kinds of heritage within which a part of school heritage can be traced back*. The *Conclusions* are the result of the collaboration between the two authors.

[27] Regarding the concept of school educational heritage, some of the most significant and recent titles relating to scientific production in the sector are reported below: Pizzigoni (2022a), Sani (2018), Meda, Cabrera, & Viñao (2017); Meda (2013); Barausse (2010); Escolano Benito (2007). Furthermore, we would like to point out the International Study Meeting *Prospettive incrociate sul Patrimonio Storico Educativo*, held at the University of Molise from 2nd to 3rd May 2018 whose acts were published in Barausse, de Freitas Ermel & Viola (2020).

the other types of heritage already legally recognised. In fact, the problem highlighted by Marta Brunelli, namely "the lack of a uniform descriptive standard that is scientifically coherent but, above all, validated by the bodies, who are responsible for coordinating the cataloguing activities of cultural heritage at national level" (Brunelli 2013, pp. 198-199), still exists ten years later[28].

Although the term school heritage was coined for the first time during the conference held by Monica Ferrari in Cremona in 2007[29], this category does not appear among those identified so far by the Italian bodies responsible for the protection and valorisation of the cultural heritage. There are several reasons for this absence. On the one hand, the difficulty of identifying school objects as heritage[30] is due to the meaning that is generally given to heritage as a group of objects not intended for consumption or not related to industrial production processes[31]. On the other hand, there is "the

---

[28] Regarding the topic of cataloguing school heritage, please also see Viola (2014). As regards teaching how to catalogue academic school museums, we propose the experience illustrated by Barausse, Andreassi, & Viola (2021).

[29] Regarding the definition of a school cultural asset, please see Ferrari, Panizza, & Morandi (2008).

[30] Under the term "historical-educational heritage" Juri Meda identifies the "system of formal tangible and/or intangible assets that have been used and/or produced in formal and/or non-formal educational contexts over time" (Meda 2013, p. 169). For the articulation of the school heritage, see pages 171-173 of the same text. For a common definition of historical-educational heritage, which includes "school historical heritage", "school cultural assets" or "cultural heritage of schools" see again Meda (2019).

[31] Meda states: "Teaching aids and school materials are generally considered as simple objects for immediate or, at most, durable consumption (if they can be used several times). For this reason, they are not usually subjected to conservation processes aimed at transforming them into full-fledged cultural assets. A set of assets subject to fragmentary and episodic conservation based on inhomogeneous criteria, in fact, has no right to be considered as a full heritage" (Meda 2013, p. 168).

multifaceted and heterogeneous nature of historical-educational heritage, whose contours are difficult to outline", as well as the recent novelty of this historiographical category (Brunelli 2013, p. 207). However, it is also true that the heuristic potential perceived in tangible sources has contributed in recent years to a greater centrality of school heritage, triggering an unstoppable process of cultural affirmation of the historical-educational heritage in general. In fact, as Roberto Sani ways, in «this new historiographical scenario» we understand how

> even the humblest tool and the simplest and most banal teaching aid inevitably acquire a specific and relevant *hermeneutic meaning*, taking on the connotation of both a *document* for reconstructing the past and a *monument* i.e. of remains and testimony. The recovery, preservation and valorisation of this heritage will make it possible to reconstruct the past (through historical research) as well as to recover and make accessible the individual and collective memory of institutions or events that can strengthen the awareness and critical conscience of individuals and communities. (Sani 2019, p. 37).

The foundation and the activity of the Italian Society for the Study of Historical-Educational Heritage (Brunelli 2017a), as well as the increase in documentation and research centres, studies and the number of opportunities for discussion among scholars represent significant stages in the process of cultural affirmation of the school historical heritage, which begun with the reflections of the French social historians Dominique Julia (1996) and Andrè Chervel (1998) in the late 1990s. Among the various promotion and valorisation initiatives linked to this line of research, the activities of the school museums play a fundamental role (Andreassi 2013), as they act as a factor in accelerating practices aimed at the necessary legal recognition of school heritage in order to subject them to appropriate protection measures[32].

The actions of school museums are aimed at disseminating the results of research for a wider public than the exclusively university one, and at satisfying the needs dictated by modern museology and the practice of the third mission of the university (Barausse & Andreassi 2019, Ascenzi & Brunelli 2020, Andreassi & Barausse 2020, Andreassi & Viola 2014). In this way, museums contribute significantly to the perception of the school heritage as a fundamental element to reconstruct the cultural identity code of the history of each individual and of the community to which they belong (D'Alessio 2020, Viola 2018b). In fact, through the activities of the museums, communities are educated to know and to recognise the objects in question as "cultural assets". Thus, the essential conditions are created for adopting the useful behaviours to prevent school heritage from being dispersed, and for carrying out the actions needed to valorise them[33].

The availability and variety of objects in their collections make school museums the leading centres for the operation and experimentation of cataloguing practices, as demonstrated by the experience of the Museum of Education in Padua, which will be the subject of a specific discussion here, starting in 2018. Among the

---

[32] Marta Brunelli has been recording a high rate of diffusion for school historical heritage museums throughout Italy since the 1990s with an acceleration after 2000, counting as many as 50 in 2018 (Brunelli 2018a, p. 15)

[33] On the educational valorisation of school heritage and museums see Brunelli (2018a); Ascenzi, Brunelli, & Meda (2019); Ascenzi, Covato, & Zago (2021); D'Alessio & Tomasco (2021). See also the experiences carried out by the school museums at the Universities of Macerata and Molise: Ascenzi & Patrizi (2014); Barausse & Andreassi (2019).

various cataloguing campaigns promoted by research centres in the field, the one in Padua is undoubtedly the main reference at the moment, particularly due to its experience as an ICCD-authorised cataloguing body. This project, which will be described in the following paragraph, represents the first general test for sectoral studies in the cataloguing managed by the central authorities. This activity is complex and not easy to understand because of the structure of the cataloguing cards, which are divided according to the fields required by the conservation needs, to be filled in according to the definitions of other scientific fields.

While awaiting the legal recognition of school collections, it is worth highlighting some of the positive effects that cataloguing (even if, at this experimental stage, it is limited by the principle of adaptation) can have for cataloguers and researchers in the sector in terms of protection and heuristic potential. In fact, the cataloguing campaigns carried out according to the parameters of the ICCD not only allowed the colleagues involved to learn a practice characterised by complex procedures and jargon outside the historical school context. It also offered the possibility of transferring the schools' historical materials to the SIGECweb online digital platform, which collects, identifies and places national cultural heritage in a protection cycle[34].

Joining the Sistema Informativo Generale del Catalogo offers numerous benefits. As with other cultural assets, adopting shared cataloguing standards enables a deep and widespread understanding of heritage. This understanding is necessary for initiating a genuine and effective protection (D'Alessio 2014) and valorisation operation, allowing for the control and limitation of its disper-

---

[34] For further information on Sistema Informativo Generale del Catalogo (SIGECweb), please refer to the next paragraph.

sion. Additionally, populating SIGECweb with descriptions of assets related to the culture of education provides the opportunity to utilise a quick and intuitive query method, offering immediate and extensive data availability. This is particularly beneficial for historians, museum and educational professionals, and cataloguers[35]. Moreover, the benefits of images and news databases for cultural assets should not be underestimated, and educational sciences should not overlook them.

For instance, consulting the SIGECweb catalogue as an art historian opens up a world of possibilities for analysis and comparison. This is crucial for a precise stylistic reading of the piece under study, unlike what happens when relying solely on study texts and catalogues from paper-based museum collections. Moreover, this tool offers support for statistical investigations, mapping, and much more (Viola 2014). These data complement and enrich the description, shedding light on the historical production context of these teaching aids[36]. Until now, they have been primarily studied through the consultation of inventories and administrative documentation within schools or commercial catalogues, published by manufacturers specializing in school education services.

The specificity of disciplinary knowledge and skills, inherent in cataloguing practice, suggests some considerations about the need for specialised training for cataloguers of school heritage. The definition of such an expert figure is urgently needed, especially we

---

[35] It is also possible to make queries for each field of the cards published in the advanced search of the General Catalogue for Cultural Assets https://catalogo.beniculturali.it/adv-search (see figure 2.4).

[36] Among the studies, which investigated the birth, diffusion and teaching use of aids, it is worth mentioning Targhetta (2020), Barausse (2020), Pizzigoni (2012 and 2015), Brunelli, 2020a and 2020b, D'Ascenzo (2020) and D'Alessio (2014).

considering that "the line of studies, such as the one on histori-cal-educational heritage, is clearly exposed to the risks of *interpre-tative indeterminacy* or, more precisely, the *loss of an effective anchoring in a historiographical context*", as Roberto Sani observed. Indeed, the tasks of recognizing, contextualizing, and producing historical information, as well as describing school heritage, which are all part of cataloguing activities, necessitate specialised training in the historical school field. This is to safeguard the school's cultural heritage from misinterpretations[37]. In fact, filling a catalogue with school historical assets presupposes basic knowledge, which can only be guaranteed by a school historian. This historian should not act as an operator, but rather as a supervisor of the catalogu-ers' work. These cataloguers should receive specific training on methodology and language, which is necessary for filling in ICCD cataloguing cards, as well as specific IT skills related to the use of the dedicated software. Therefore, a scientific supervision and that multidisciplinary approach, which was invoked by Monica Ferrari at the conference on school heritage in Cremona in 2007, must be guaranteed to cataloguers:

> Enhancing school heritage also means constructing cultural
> skills, taste and sensitivity, that is, a new scientific commu-
> nity, who is among history, pedagogy and much more,
> inaugurating an "ecological" perspective, which allows us

---

[37] "In fact, as it has emerged from some studies, which have recently ap-peared in the international scenario, the temptation is to replace the *strictly historiographical approach* (it is certainly very demanding!) with an *anthro-pological, ethnological, semiotic approach*, etc., which inevitably tends to lose the awareness that only an authentically historical reading of school educa-tional heritage can give us the most authentic meaning of such a heritage. Hence, the choice to place a sort of *methodological prejudicial question* or, better to say, a precise reference to the real centrality of a *historiographical approach* at the centre of our reflection" (Sani, 2019, p. 40).

to understand some of the relationships between micro- and macro-system starting from the new ongoing network of knowledge (Ferrari, Panizza, & Morandi 2008, p. 26).

This rapid introduction is coming to an end and aims at contributing to show how the intricate network of knowledge has become increasingly dense also thanks to SIPSE contribution and its committees.

Comparative analysis of existing ICCD cataloguing cards, referring to those kinds of heritage within which a part of school heritage can be traced

First of all, in dealing with the comparative analysis of cataloguing cards, the subject of this study, it is necessary to point out that the general national catalogue of cultural assets is created and managed by ICCD through SIGECweb platform[38], which represents an effective working tool and a safe method for the production of Cataloguing Cards in a single homogeneous area as it is a unitary transversal information system among different kinds of assets.

Cataloguing Cards are organised based on 30 different disciplinary fields to which they belong and have been defined up to now: each of them has its own identifying code (A, BDM, OA, RA, PST, etc.) and a corresponding definition indicating its application field (Mancinelli 2018).

---

[38] A *web-based* platform manages the whole cataloguing flow, which can be reached at: <http://www.sigecweb.beniculturali.it/it.iccd.sigec.axweb. Main/>; access to the system is allowed to register users, who are associated with an accredited body; for all the indications: <http://www. iccd. beniculturali.it/it/Catalogazione> (01.11. 2022).

settore disciplinare	sigla	definizione	categoria
beni archeologici	AT	Reperti antropologici	beni mobili
	CA	Complessi archeologici	beni immobili
	MA	Monumenti archeologici	beni immobili
	RA	Reperti archeologici	beni mobili
	SAS	Saggi stratigrafici	beni immobili
	SI	Siti archeologici	beni immobili
	TMA	Tabella materiali archeologici	beni mobili
beni architettonici e paesaggistici	A	Architettura	beni immobili
	CNS	Centri/nuclei storici	beni immobili
	PG	Parchi/giardini	beni immobili
beni demoetnoantropologici	BDI	Beni demoetnoantropologici immateriali	beni immateriali
	BDM	Beni demoetnoantropologici materiali	beni mobili
beni fotografici	F	Fotografia	beni mobili
	FF	Fondi fotografici	beni mobili
beni musicali	SM	Strumenti musicali	beni mobili
	SMO	Strumenti musicali-Organo	beni mobili
beni naturalistici	BNB	Beni naturalistici-Botanica	beni mobili
	BNM	Beni naturalistici-Mineralogia	beni mobili
	BNP	Beni naturalistici-Paleontologia	beni mobili
	BNPE	Beni naturalistici-Petrologia	beni mobili
	BNPL	Beni naturalistici-Planetologia	beni mobili
	BNZ	Beni naturalistici-Zoologia	beni mobili
beni numismatici	NU	Beni numismatici	beni mobili
beni scientifici e tecnologici	PST	Patrimonio scientifico e tecnologico	beni mobili
beni storici e artistici	D	Disegni	beni mobili
	MI	Matrici incise	beni mobili
	OA	Opere/oggetti d'arte	beni mobili
	OAC	Opere/oggetti d'arte contemporanea	beni mobili
	S	Stampe	beni mobili
	VeAC	Vestimenti antichi/contemporanei	beni mobili

Pic. 2.1. *Disciplinary fields of the card in SIGECweb*

The standards, which were defined by ICCD for each card, have undergone updates and modifications linked to progress and refinement of scientific research in various disciplinary fields over time, as well as the increasingly complex and articulated cataloguing needs, which have led to develop subsequent "versions" of different cataloguing cards (version 1.00, 2.00, 3.00, 3.01; version 4.00 is currently the latest one).

Since such a national cataloguing lacks a specific attention to the set of cultural assets relating to the variegated school world, it is proposed to use the cards, which are already available, until an *ad hoc* cataloguing card for school historical heritage is prepared. For this reason, a comparative analysis was carried out between the kinds of school heritage and ICCD cataloguing cards in SIGECweb in order to identify univocal criteria for cataloguing that part of the heritage, which can be catalogued at least.

The analysis was carried out by the Education Museum at the University of Padua, which has been using SIGECweb platform for cataloguing for some years like other university museums and, therefore, it was possible for it to take place with tests and experimentations on real materials.

After a careful study, they identified a field in all the cataloguing cards, which are available in version 4.00 (but also in all the versions included in SIGECweb), and it can be used to identify school heritage.

This is the ATB paragraph (Cultural Area or Production Area) where various indications relating to the cultural area to which the catalogued asset refers must be included. This paragraph is made up of different fields and is repetitive in order to record data relating to different cultural areas, which may be involved. Therefore, its use, which we can define as "unorthodox", would allow school materials to be easily identified, even if they are catalogued in cards relating to different kinds of assets.

There are two fields, which must be filled in, because they have a mandatory context according to ICCD directives, i.e. by entering information in the first one, it is necessary to also fill in the second one. The first one is ATBD (Denomination) for which the law provides: «Indicating the cultural area. Definitions will be used, such as area, culture, period, production, school, manufacturing, etc.; these terms will be followed by the geographical qualification or the name of area, culture, period, production, school, manufacturing, etc. Open vocabulary [the content of the vocabulary may vary in relation to the kind of card and the specific disciplinary application field]» (Mancinelli 2017, pp. 121-122). The second field to be filled in is ATBM (Reason/source) for which the law provides: «Indicating the elements determining the attribution to the cultural area proposed. Closed vocabulary; refer to Appendix III for filling in» (*ibid.*, p. 122).

On the SIGECweb platform, there is the possibility of including only the information, which has been already preloaded (a sort of "drop-down" menu), for fields with closed vocabulary.

Therefore, in order to catalogue school heritage so that they are easily identifiable, it is necessary to enter ATBD (Denomination): "School Area" and ATBM (Reason): "Typological analysis" or "Documentation", depending on the cases.

The analysis revealed that there are some different kinds of materials in the historical school heritage for which it is sufficient to enter the above-mentioned information in the two fields in order to be able to easily identify them as school heritage. It deals with:

- materials to be catalogued with card PST (Technical-Scientific Heritage), consisting of school collections with scientific tools and technological devices (including radios, projectors, record players, etc.), an example of such a card is in figure 2.5;

- school collections with aids, which were used for teaching natural sciences (stuffed animals, collections of minerals and fossils, herbariums, etc.), in order to be catalogued using the card relating to a specific asset, i.e. BNB (Naturalistic-Botanical Heritage), BNM (Naturalistic Mineralogical Heritage), BNP (Naturalistic-Paleontological Heritage), BNPE (Naturalistic Petrological Heritage), BNPL (Naturalistic Planetological Heritage), BNZ (Naturalistic Zoological Heritage);

- school collections of musical assets, i.e. the set of equipment and aids (musical instruments, tuning forks, metronomes, etc.), which were used for teaching music and have to be catalogued with card SM (Musical Instruments);

- photographic funds relating to the school world to be catalogued with card F (Photographical Heritage);

- school numismatic collections, i.e. coins and other numismatic objects (including seals and medals belonging to any era), to be catalogued with card NU (Numismatic Heritage);

- diplomas, certificates and wall posters relating to the school world to be catalogued using card S (Printed materials).

Pic. 2.2. *Materials similar to the school ones, which are catalogued with cards BNZ, SM, F, NU, S (from the General Catalogue of Cultural Heritage)*

Pic. 2.3. *Geographical, gymnastic, pedagogical materials and furnishings, which are catalogued in BDM (from the General Catalogue of Cultural Heritage)*

When it comes to other types of school materials, the comparative analysis with today's cards was much more complex. This led to a temporary evaluation using the card BDM (Demo-ethno-anthropological Heritage) – for compatible assets. However, its use was enforced not only by filling the fields requested for the school area, as with other cards, but also by entering a new lemma.

This is necessary because card BDM in version 4.00 provides for obligatorily filling in field CTG – Category with values, which can be exclusively entered from a closed two-level vocabulary (Tucci 2017, pp. 18, 57-61) –, unlike other cards. Among these values, there is currently no lemma, which can be used in a not too arbitrary way.

Therefore, ICCD will have to be officially asked to include a new lemma relating to the second level of "Furniture and Furnishings" in a closed vocabulary to be added to the one in "Containers and objects for domestic use", also providing the one for "school use".

Otherwise, you could only ask to modify the lemma in: "Containers and objects for domestic and school use".

It should be noted that there are not all these problems relating to the category of an asset in card BDM in version 2.00 where the field has an open vocabulary instead and, therefore, the cataloguing proposal can be already immediately used on SIGECweb.

By filling in both the fields related to the school area and those related to the asset category with a new lemma, it would be possible to catalogue the following assets (identified by Meda 2010) using the BDM card:

- school collections with mathematical and/or geometric materials consisting of all the equipment and the aids, which were used for teaching Maths and Geometry (nomograms, abacuses and other calculation tools, slide rulers and number cards, wooden, metal, paper and/or plastic geometric models, etc.), an example of such a card is in figure 2.6;

- school collections with geographical materials, i.e., the set of equipment and aids, which were used for teaching Geography (world maps, planetariums, geographical maps, etc.);

- collections with gymnastic materials, i.e., gymnastic equipment, which was used in Physical Education (Indian clubs, hoops, sticks, ropes, wall bars, etc.);

- various kinds of pedagogical materials, which were developed within particular teaching methods and used within schools (Froebelian gifts, Montessorian cognitive development materials, alphabet blocks with movable types and sensory alphabet blocks, etc.);

– tangible materials, which have been stratified within schools over time: furnishings, stationery, writing tools, objects belonging to pupils' kit, etc.

– Even school furniture can be catalogued with the same card BDM because there is already the lemma "Furniture", just as there is already the category "Clothes and body ornaments", which can be used for school clothing (Tucci 2017, pp. 58-59).

– However, there is no ICCD cataloguing card, which can be used at least in a sensible way, for a large number of school materials. In particular, it concerns:

– exercise books;

– teaching papers (including articles produced after learning processes, which were induced by means of pedagogical materials);

– school reports;

– the so-called school film strips (since they are audiovisual materials, they could be included among what will be catalogued in the future according to the new bibliographic standards, which are being currently studied).

It should be noted that school heritage for which there is no problem for ICCD cataloguing, i.e., architectural and artistic assets, have not been taken into account in the analysis, while there are already other legally recognized forms of cataloguing book and archival assets.

At the end of the analysis introduced here, the result we have reached is that of having identified an overall simple method to allow a large part of school historical heritage to be catalogued, even in the absence of a specific disciplinary field, which is recognized by ICCD. At the same time, the kinds of school materials, which remain excluded from the current possibilities for national cataloguing, have been focused and this is the problem, which remains open.

Conclusions

The analysis, which has been carried out so far, does not certainly aim at submitting definitive results of an ongoing experience, but rather illustrating the first advances, which were made in the cataloguing field, within the broader protection, promotion and valorisation process of historical-educational heritage. Therefore, the intent here is to illustrate the state of art of an experimentation with various elements of complexity, which are attributable to new skills required to those who directly work for protecting cultural assets, on the one hand, and the continuous revision process to which it is subjected due to the continuous urging requests coming from both the studies on historical-educational heritage and the principles and rules on cataloguing, on the other hand.

In conclusion, the contribution aims at offering the scientific community a punctual report on the work, which has been carried out so far, in order to update and enrich the reflection on the topic of school historical heritage, which is becoming increasingly complex with new elements. Instead, the proposals, which have been put forward in this contribution, can be a tool, which allows the operators in the field to catalogue a part of the school historical assets at least in some way.

The activity will continue with the already planned future steps, which will be added to this current analysis, i.e., even the study and development of what will be necessary to achieve the recognition of a long-awaited *ad hoc* cataloguing card for school historical heritage by ICCD, in addition to the presentation of results.

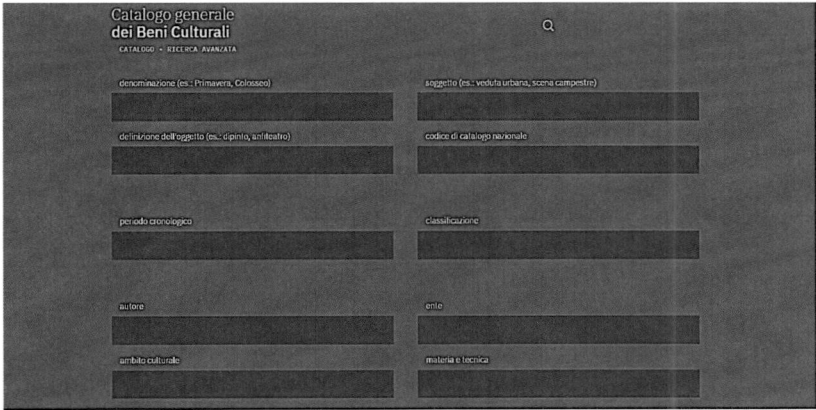

Pic. 2.4. *Screenshot relating to the Advanced Search in the General Catalogue of Cultural Assets where there is also the "cultural area" field (<https://catalogo.benic-ulturali.it/adv-search>)*

Pic. 2.5. *PST cataloguing card relating to a projector for film strips and slides, which was processed on SIGECweb and had been already published in the General Catalogue of Cultural Heritage (pp 1-4) (<https://catalogo.beniculturali.it/detail/ScientificOrTechnologicalHeritage/ 0500695584>)*

PVCL - Località	PADOVA
LDC - COLLOCAZIONE SPECIFICA	
LDCT - Tipologia	museo
LDCQ - Qualificazione	universitario
LDCN - Denominazione attuale	Palazzo ECA (ex)
LDCU - Indirizzo	Via degli Obizzi, 21-23
LDCM - Denominazione raccolta	Museo dell'Educazione dell'Università degli Studi di Padova
LDCS - Specifiche	Collezione sussidi didattici
UB - UBICAZIONE E DATI PATRIMONIALI	
INV - INVENTARIO	
INVD - Data	
INVN - Numero	
LA - ALTRE LOCALIZZAZIONI GEOGRAFICO-AMMINISTRATIVE	
TCL - Tipo di localizzazione	luogo di esposizione
PRV - LOCALIZZAZIONE GEOGRAFICO-AMMINISTRATIVA	
PRVS - Stato	ITALIA
PRVR - Regione	Veneto
PRVP - Provincia	PD
PRVC - Comune	Padova
DT - CRONOLOGIA	
DTZ - CRONOLOGIA GENERICA	
DTZG - Fascia cronologica di riferimento	XX secolo
DTZS - Frazione cronologica	secondo quarto
DTS - CRONOLOGIA SPECIFICA	
DTSI - Da	1940
DTSV - Validità	ca
DTSF - A	1950
DTM - Motivazione cronologia	analisi tipologica
AU - DEFINIZIONE CULTURALE	
ATB - AMBITO CULTURALE	
ATBD - Denominazione	ambito scolastico

ATBM - Motivazione dell''attribuzione	analisi tipologica
MT - DATI TECNICI	
MTC - Materia e tecnica	ghisa, bachelite, vetro / assemblaggio
MIS - MISURE	
MISU - Unità	cm
MISA - Altezza	18
MISL - Larghezza	26
MISN - Lunghezza	11
DA - DATI ANALITICI	
DES - DESCRIZIONE	
DESO - Oggetto	Proiettore per filmine e diapositive 35mm, con alloggiamento della lampada in ghisa di colore verde e lenti Lumen Parvum F 85. Prodotto dalla Soc. La Scuola di Brescia per essere usato nelle scuole, soprattutto elementari, per le proiezioni delle cosiddette "filmine scolastiche" con immagini fisse relative alle più diverse materie.
UTF - Funzione	didattico-educativa
UTM - Modalità d'uso	L'apparecchio proiettava immagini fisse su pellicola o su diapositiva a seconda del supporto inserito; la luce proveniva da una lampada interna accesa elettricamente
STM - STEMMI, EMBLEMI, MARCHI	
STMC - Classe di appartenenza	stemma
STMQ - Qualificazione	commerciale
STMU - Quantità	1
STMP - Posizione	sul lato sinistro
STMD - Descrizione	SOC. LA SCUOLA-BRESCIA
CO - CONSERVAZIONE	
STC - STATO DI CONSERVAZIONE	
STCC - Stato di conservazione	buono
TU - CONDIZIONE GIURIDICA E VINCOLI	
ACQ - ACQUISIZIONE	
ACQT - Tipo acquisizione	dato non disponibile
ACQD - Data acquisizione	n.d.
CDG - CONDIZIONE GIURIDICA	
CDGG - Indicazione	

generica	proprietà Ente pubblico non territoriale
CDGS - Indicazione specifica	Università degli Studi di Padova
DO - FONTI E DOCUMENTI DI RIFERIMENTO	
FTA - DOCUMENTAZIONE FOTOGRAFICA	
FTAX - Genere	documentazione allegata
FTAP - Tipo	fotografia digitale (file)
FTAN - Codice identificativo	UniPd_MdE00695584_00065F
AD - ACCESSO AI DATI	
ADS - SPECIFICHE DI ACCESSO AI DATI	
ADSP - Profilo di accesso	1
ADSM - Motivazione	scheda contenente dati liberamente accessibili
CM - COMPILAZIONE	
CMP - COMPILAZIONE	
CMPD - Data	
CMPN - Nome	
RSR - Referente scientifico	
FUR - Funzionario responsabile	

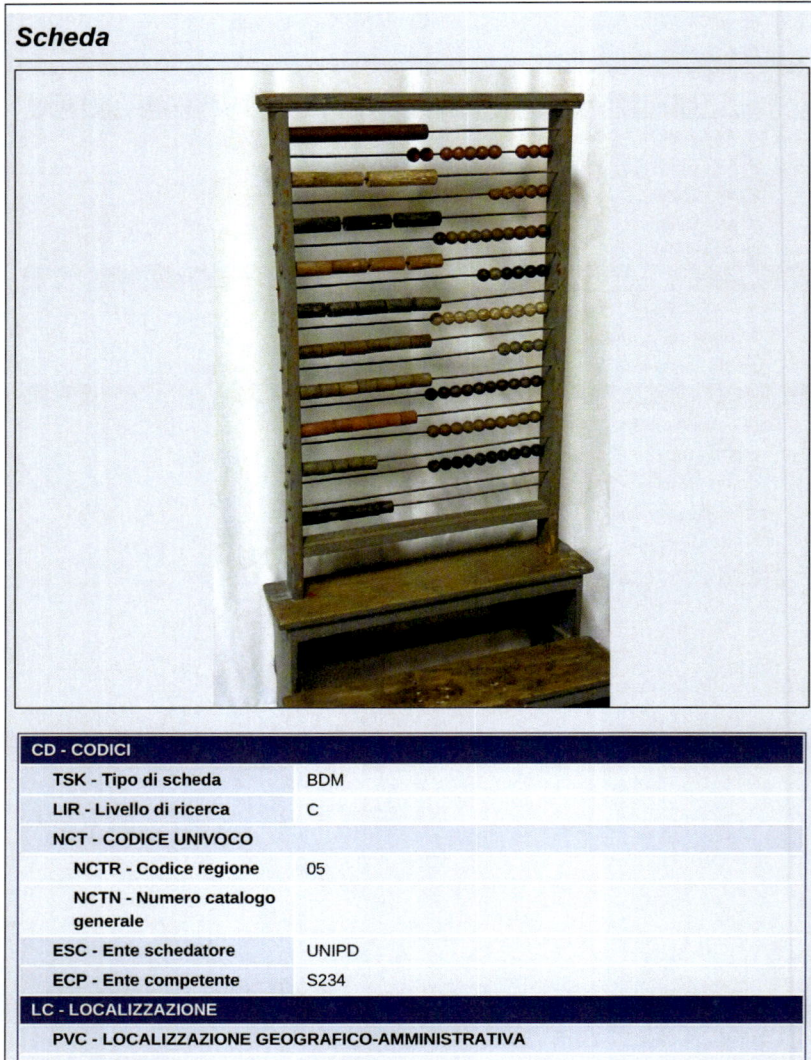

Scheda	
CD - CODICI	
TSK - Tipo di scheda	BDM
LIR - Livello di ricerca	C
NCT - CODICE UNIVOCO	
NCTR - Codice regione	05
NCTN - Numero catalogo generale	
ESC - Ente schedatore	UNIPD
ECP - Ente competente	S234
LC - LOCALIZZAZIONE	
PVC - LOCALIZZAZIONE GEOGRAFICO-AMMINISTRATIVA	
PVCS - Stato	ITALIA

Pic. 2.6. *BDM 2.00 cataloguing card relating to an abacus, which was processed on SIGECweb and had been already published in the General Catalogue of Cultural Heritage (pages 1-4). (<https://catalogo.beniculturali.it/detail/DemoEthnoAnthropologicalHeritage/0500695674>)*

PVCP - Provincia	PD	
PVCC - Comune	Padova	
PVCL - Località	PADOVA	
LDC - COLLOCAZIONE SPECIFICA		
LDCT - Tipologia	museo	
LDCQ - Qualificazione	universitario	
LDCN - Denominazione attuale	Palazzo ECA (ex)	
LDCU - Indirizzo	Via degli Obizzi, 21-23	
LDCM - Denominazione raccolta	Museo dell'Educazione dell'Università degli Studi di Padova	
LDCS - Specifiche	Sala V	
UB - UBICAZIONE		
INV - INVENTARIO DI MUSEO O DI COLLEZIONE		
INVN - Numero		
INVD - Data		
LA - ALTRE LOCALIZZAZIONI		
TCL - Tipo di localizzazione	di archivio	
PRV - LOCALIZZAZIONE GEOGRAFICO-AMMINISTRATIVA		
PRVS - Stato	ITALIA	
PRVR - Regione	Veneto	
PRVP - Provincia	PD	
PRVC - Comune	Padova	
OG - OGGETTO		
OGT - DEFINIZIONE DELL'OGGETTO		
OGTD - Definizione	pallottoliere	
OGTG - Definizione della categoria generale	arredi e suppellettili	
OGTE - Definizione della categoria specifica	contenitori, recipienti e oggetti di uso scolastico	
OGTT - Tipologia specifica	frazioniere	
QNT - Quantità	1	
AU - AUTORE FABBRICAZIONE/ ESECUZIONE		
ATB - AMBITO DI PRODUZIONE		
ATBD - Denominazione	ambito scolastico	
ATBM - Motivazione	analisi tipologica	

DTF - CRONOLOGIA DI FABBRICAZIONE/ ESECUZIONE	
DTFZ - Datazione	fine XVIII - inizio XIX secolo
DTFM - Motivazione della datazione	analisi tipologica
MT - DATI TECNICI	
MTC - MATERIA E TECNICA	
MTCM - Materia	legno
MTCT - Tecnica	inchiodatura
MTC - MATERIA E TECNICA	
MTCM - Materia	ferro
MTCT - Tecnica	incastro
MIS - MISURE	
MISU - Unità	cm
MISA - Altezza	166
MISL - Larghezza	79
MISS - Spessore	40
UT - USO	
UTF - Funzione	didattica
CO - CONSERVAZIONE	
STC - STATO DI CONSERVAZIONE	
STCC - Dati di conservazione	discreto
STCS - Indicazioni specifiche	Sono mancanti alcuni cilindri del frazioniere e alcune palline del pallottoliere.
DA - DATI ANALITICI	
DES - DESCRIZIONE	
DESO - Indicazioni sull'oggetto	Pallottoliere-frazioniere in legno e ferro, verniciato di colore grigio. Privo delle gambe originali, è oggi ancorato ad una di quelle scalette utilizzate per consentire ai bambini più piccoli di scrivere alla lavagna. Consta di palline e di cilindri in legno che scorrono in aste di ferro. Palline e cilindri svolgono funzioni diverse: le prime possono essere utilizzate come un classico pallottoliere, mentre i secondi servono per l'insegnamento delle frazioni e costituiscono il frazioniere vero e proprio. Quest'ultimo è così composto: un cilindro scorrevole inserito nella prima asta di ferro in alto rappresenta l'unità, i cilindri successivi sono tutti eguali in lunghezza, ma di differenti colori e divisi rispettivamente in due, in tre, in quattro, fino in dieci parti eguali. Con questo strumento gli insegnanti avevano facile modo di far

	vedere ai bambini il diverso valore delle frazioni e i rapporti di queste fra loro. Una antica testimonianza di questo sussidio è data da Ferrante Aporti nel 1833.
TU - CONDIZIONE GIURIDICA E VINCOLI	
ACQ - ACQUISIZIONE	
ACQT - Tipo di acquisizione	donazione
ACQN - Nome	Scuola elementare
ACQD - Data	1994
ACQL - Luogo di acquisizione	Gaiba (RO)
CDG - CONDIZIONE GIURIDICA	
CDGG - Indicazione generica	proprietà Ente pubblico non territoriale
CDGS - Indicazione specifica	Università degli Studi di Padova
DO - FONTI E DOCUMENTI DI RIFERIMENTO	
FTA - DOCUMENTAZIONE FOTOGRAFICA	
FTAX - Genere	specifiche allegate
FTAP - Tipo	fotografia digitale (file)
FTAN - Codice identificativo	UniPd_MdE00695674_0001F
BIB - BIBLIOGRAFIA	
BIBX - Genere	di confronto
BIBA - Autore	Aporti, Ferrante
BIBD - Anno di edizione	1833
BIBI - Volume, tavole, figure	Tav. I
BIBH - Sigla per citazione	00001112
CM - COMPILAZIONE	
CMP - COMPILAZIONE	
CMPD - Data	
CMPN - Nome	
FUR - Funzionario responsabile	
RVM - TRASCRIZIONE	
RVMD - Data	
RVMN - Nome	

Chapter 3

Exercise books among Research, Teaching and Third Mission: Some Reflections in View of a Cataloguing Protocol

by Francesca Borruso

Preface

No ICCD cataloguing card, which can be used in a congruous and adequate way for various possible implications relating to both research and teaching activities, has been formalised up to now for exercise books belonging to the heritage of school life and currently included among demo-ethno-anthropological cultural assets or even simply among historical assets – as it is well illustrated in the essay in this volume by Valeria Viola and Mara Orlando. The necessity to provide in this sense is linked to a multiplicity of cultural needs, designing an ad hoc cataloguing card.

Firstly, this choice would be desirable in relation to a preservation policy of the documents in their material integrity: in fact, as it is known, most of the school archives are in conditions of neglect in school basements or are intentionally destroyed in some cases, due to the lack of space and resources, which are adequate for their conservation (Meda 2013). In the absence of a detailed regulatory protection on cataloguing documents, even the creation of a widespread educational process, which is aimed at respecting this specific cultural asset, would always remain difficult to achieve. In fact, as it is known, legal provisions also fulfill an educational function, which is aimed at orienting the partners' behaviours and generating sensitivity, care, and attention, which could otherwise remain completely unrealised. Secondly, the identification of an *ad hoc* cataloguing card would make documents more usable and traceable within various research paths, which are mainly historical-educational, but not only, and are increasingly emerging over the last years[39]. Furthermore, a cataloguing card would prove useful both within school and university teaching experience and within research training, which is carried out with young PhD students and scholars, since consultation and access to sources has an indisputable and unreplaceable relevance in all the training processes[40].

Within the recent 2nd National Congress with Società Italiana per lo studio del Patrimonio Storico-Educativo (SIPSE), which took place in Padua on 7th and 8th October 2021, there were many testimonies relating to the pedagogical use of books in the past, which are preserved in School Museums or other institutional archives and have proven to be precious for mainly teaching history, but also in the context of education for the protection of cultural heritage and civic education *tout court*, with primary and secondary school students. The teaching projects, which emerged during the above-mentioned conference, were essentially aimed at building a culture, which was focused on the valorisation of documentary heritage, the knowledge and acquisition of cataloguing processes

---

[39] See Sani (2018). See also the recent volume edited by Ascenzi, Covato, & Zago (2021).

[40] For the relevance of the archives, which can be consulted in the field of school teaching, see Fogliardi & Marcadella (2010).

and the hermeneutic-critical interpretation of the most disparate historical-educational documents[41].

Additionally, in this perspective, there is a growing focus on ancient or new school museums. In particular, school museums often possess a significant historical-cultural heritage, such as archives, bibliographies, or object-related collections. These museums offer opportunities for research, curricular and extracurricular teaching, and scientific dissemination activities, primarily within the context of university departments (Borruso & Cantatore 2021b). These structures – which originally emerged to support the birth of the public education system[42] – today are intended to preserve the educational memory of schools. Moreover, they currently align perfectly with the University's Third Mission (Frondizi 2020), which promotes collaboration, dialogue, dissemination, and scientific and cultural exchange between universities and their territories. This demonstrates the value of scientific research within community life and the fruitful circulation of ideas and knowledge.

---

[41] Many interventions in that direction are part of recently published Conference Proceedings. Among them, I mention the essay by Giorgi (2021).

[42] About the history of MuSEd see Borruso, Cantatore, & Covato (2020), Cantatore (2019) and Sanzo (2020).

Pic. 3.1 *Funds for MuSEd – Museo della Scuola e dell' Educazione 'Mauro Laeng', Department of Education, Roma Tre University, exhibition hall.*

Pic. 3.2. *MuSEd. Museo della Scuola e dell' Educazione 'Mauro Laeng', Department of Education, Roma Tre University, exhibition hall.*

Pic. 3.3. *Secondary school students visiting the MuSEd, Department of Educational Sciences, Roma Tre University, original rural school desks coming from Val D'Orcia, 1920s.*

The increasingly widespread experience of Public History (AIPH 2018, https://aiph.hypotheses.org/>) is part of the Third University Mission, which involves forms of historical dissemination carried out outside academic environments. In this context, school museums are recognised as privileged places for a variety of initiatives aimed not only at disseminating knowledge, but also at fostering local training opportunities and promoting research and shared building paths for historical knowledge, involving individuals, groups and communities 'from below' (Noiret 2015, Ridolfi 2017, Portelli 2017, Carrattieri 2020). This multiplicity of training paths also refers to the new idea of value for cultural heritage, which is closely linked to its real accessibility and usability by citizens and must be increasingly broad and democratic: this concept is in the Faro Convention and was signed by Italy in 2013 (Feliciati 2015, Yanes Cabrera 2011). Such accessibility to cultural heritage does not turn into the simple dissemination of information or knowledge, but it should be translated into a pedagogical-educational choice, which is focused on an active interaction with the public (Bertuccelli 2017) who is involved in a shared path of historical reasoning. In the context of school history, a Public History of this kind implies as an indispensable prerequisite the access to a school heritage that also includes exercise books, privileged witnesses of the controversial and complex real educational processes.

Exercise books and historical-educational research

We know that the use of exercise books on a large scale in Europe can only be traced back to the mid-nineteenth century. It was an important event, which contributed to influencing the processes of school literacy, making them more widespread throughout the territory, more rooted among people, and more uniform in terms of study contents and methods used[43].

---

[43] "However, documentary sources do not allow us to establish a real history of exercise books today. While we documented their existence in a non-negligible part of classes from 1833, it is only since 1860, when their practice was really widespread, that we have found a sufficient corpus of them in preserved collections" (Hébrard 1995, p. 147).

Thus, as a witness to school educational practices in Italy especially starting from the post-unification age onwards, the exercise
book has been a specificity of the documentary heritage, which has
been widely used by historical-educational research for several
decades (Sani 2012). First of all, it proved precious in the context
of new frontiers for annalist historical-educational research (Burke
2014), which must necessarily be addressed to atypical sources, "in
spite of themselves", according to Marc Bloch's famous definition
(Bloch 1981), as they are engaged in reconstructing total or partial
history, giving visibility to new unparalleled topics and subjects in
the historiographical reconstruction[44]. In short, these sources were
not born as historical sources, but they can become in this way,
in spite of themselves: now, this consideration has been acquired
and has significantly expanded not only the phenomenology of
sources, but it has also made them an open and continuously
growing system[45].

Within history of pedagogy and education, this change tried to
overcome the traditional history of pedagogical ideas – which was
the study of doctrines and systems of thoughts – in order to turn
the attention to the unravelling of concrete – intentional and informal – educational and training processes, which are intertwined
not only with history of ideas, but also with history of educational
and training institutions and even broader socio-cultural changes[46].

Already Dominique Julia (1996) highlighted the need to investigate school material culture, which was still valued in histori-

[44] For this topic, see Cambi (2004) and Sani (2016).
[45] For the atypical nature of historical sources, see Ginzburg (1992 and 2000)
and, yet, Farge (2003).
[46] For this change, it is considered emblematic the volume by Egle Becchi
(1987); and yet, see *Storia sociale dell'educazione. Modelli e problemi*, monographic issue of "Studi sulla formazione" (Cambi 2004).

cal-educational research too little and, instead, able to find a new school history and educational life, which would have given visibility to little known topics, questions and subjects. This educational materiality would have required new sources: from textbooks (Chiosso 2000) to teaching tools, which were really used, from the analysis of spaces and places of school life to students' school supplies. In short, exercise books have mostly emerged as specific sources allowing us to reconstruct aspects of educational micro-history, which are difficult to find in other documents (Escolano Benito 2005).

Pic. 3.4 *Exercise book from Montesca school (Città di Castello, Umbria), 1920s, MuSEd, Department of Educational Sciences, Roma Tre University*

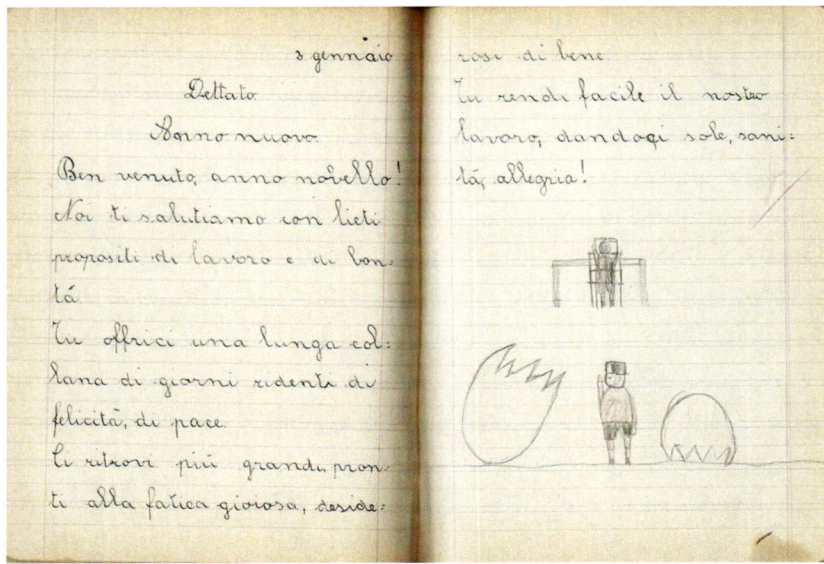

Pic. 3.5 *Primary school exercise book, 1930s, MuSEd, Department of Educational Sciences, Roma Tre University*

In recent years, many research lines have also investigated exercise books, which are becoming precious for studying school practices, teaching contents, the interplay between theory and educational practices, more or less innovative teaching methods across diverse disciplines, and school governance rules and objectives. For example, through exercise books, it was possible to study the extent of school propaganda invasiveness, a practice employed by dictatorial regimes[47], as well as the disciplinary and control mechanisms in institutional life: from the system of rewards and punishments to teaching evaluation systems.

---

[47] See the section *Propaganda. The Exercise Book as a Tool of Mass Communication*, which contains a plurality of studies on the relationship between exercise books and state propaganda, in Meda, Montino, & Sani (2010), pp. 211-471.

However, not only information relating to school life, but also information linked to the broader life and existential field of children can emerge from exercise books. For example, this information may concern family lifestyles, educational practices, which were widespread in certain contexts, childhood living conditions and bringing up methods, child labour, rural life, migratory phenomena, gender educational differences and the girls' living conditions, infant mortality, hygienic-sanitary conditions, dominant mentalities, the imagination of a community and so on (Certini 2001, pp. 200 ff.).

Pic. 3.6. *(on the left) Reproduction of an exercise book cover from the 1930s, MuSEd, Department of Educational Sciences, Roma Tre University; Pic. 7. (on the right) MuSEd, Department of Educational Sciences, Roma Tre University*

This wide-ranging plurality of information is related to the socio-cultural conditions belonging to the children's writing: thus, school culture can be understood in its connections with broader social-historical phenomenologies, from history of ideas to history of daily life, imagination (Montino 2006, pp. 167-168), emotions, mentalities, educational practices and so on (Meda 2006b, p. 75). It is true that exercise books were mainly created within institutional contexts and were therefore mostly controlled, guided and super-vised by adults (Meda 2006a, p. 287), which is why Hébrard noted that "there is a great lack of draft exercise books in the archives" (Hébrard 1995, p. 150). Nevertheless, they can sometimes reveal truly authentic «children's writings» from which it seems possible to intercept those 'children's voices' that are difficult to find even in family archives. The authenticity of children's expression is a diffi-cult topic to be decoded since exercise books are generally consid-ered as historical documents, which were subject to adults' inter-vention/control, but it is also rarely possible to perceive children's writings in their authorship (Gibelli 2012). In fact, within Mauro Laeng School and Education Museum, there are also valuable collections of exercise books[48] testifying a greater expressive free-dom, which was granted to students in some forms of pedagogical experimentation, which were carried out by little-known country teachers. As part of his idea of a serene school (Lombardo Radice 1925), Giuseppe Lombardo Radice recommended that teachers left children free during the class composition without any instruction for a rigid outline, as practiced in traditional schools[49].

---

[48] Mauro Laeng School and Education Museum at the Department of Edu-cational Sciences in Roma Tre University preserves several collections of exercise books. Containing 159 collections of primary exercise books, Lom-bardo Radice Educational Archive is particularly valuable and interesting. See Borruso (2010 and 2018).

[49] See Cantatore (2020). For the instruction relating to the free composition and the creation of the living book built by children, see Cantatore (2010).

Pic. 3.8. *Lombardo Radice Educational Archive, MuSEd, Department of Educational Sciences, Roma Tre University, primary school of Sassari, Sardinia, Teacher Olga Raffaelli, school year 1936-1937*

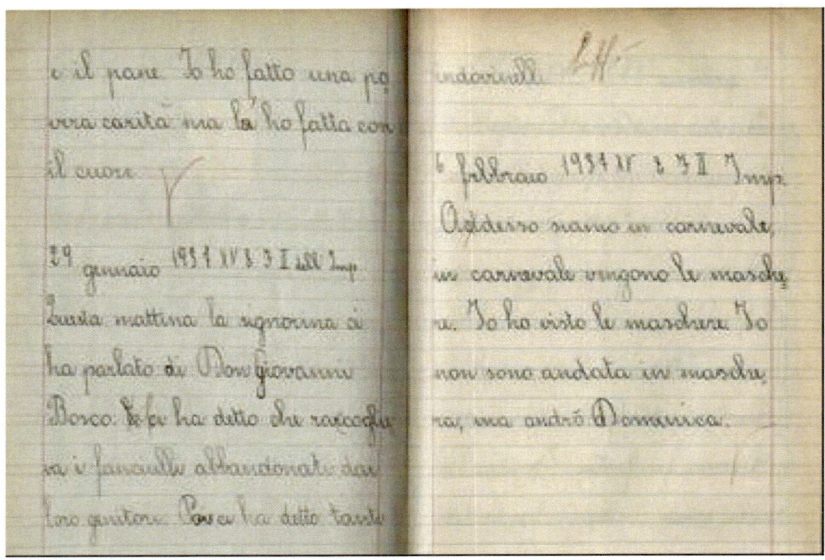

Pic. 3.9. *Exercise book belonging to a third-grade child, Belluno, school year 1936-37, MuSEd, Department of Educational Sciences, Roma Tre University*

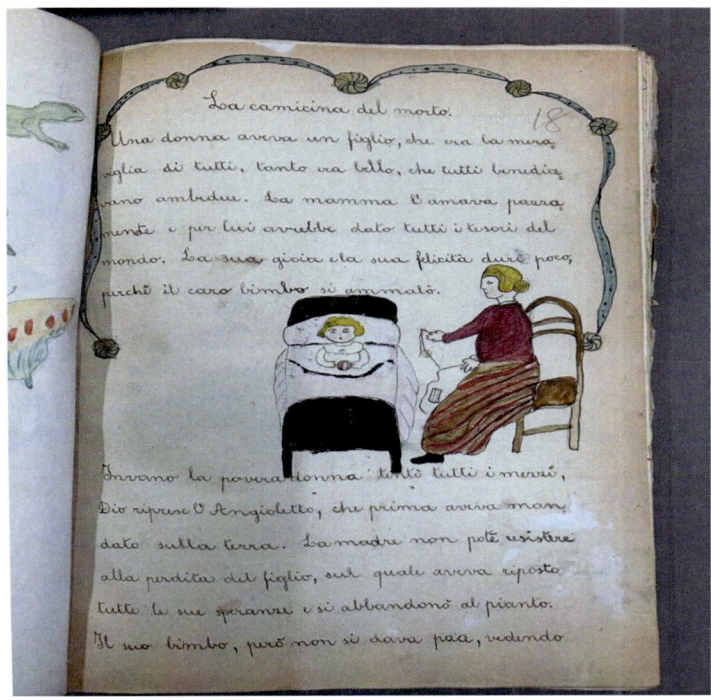

Pic. 3.10. *Lombardo Radice Educational Archive, MuSEd, Department of Educational Sciences, Roma Tre University, primary school of Sassari, Sardinia, Teacher Olga Raffaelli, school year 1936-1937*

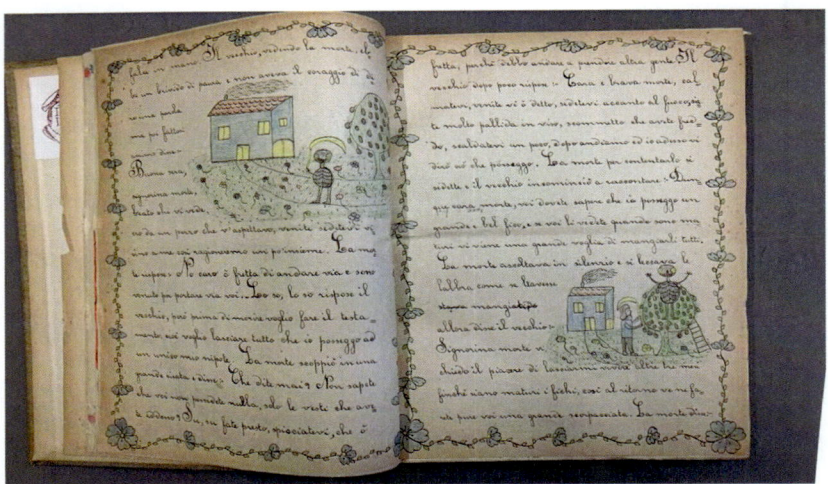

Pic. 3.11. *Lombardo Radice Didactic Archive, MuSEd, Department of Education Sciences, Roma Tre University, Elementary school of Sassari, Sardinia, Teacher Olga Raffaelli, school year 1936-1937*

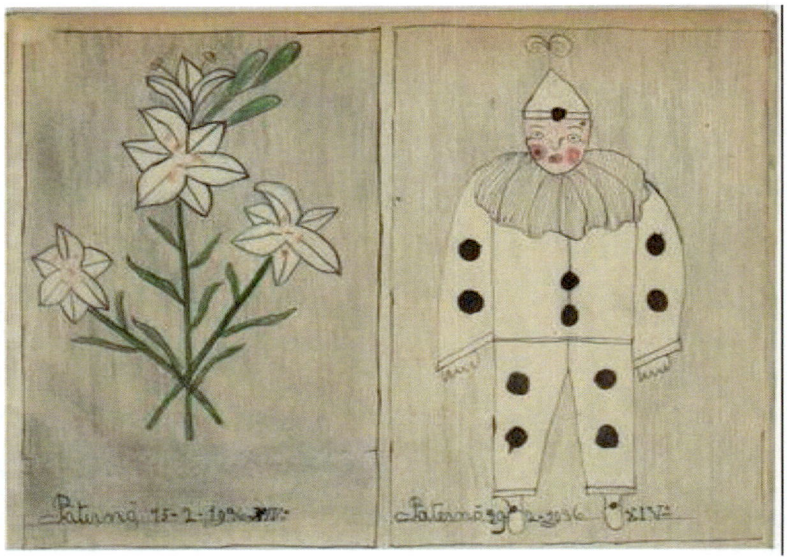

Pic. 3.12. *Sketchbook, Belluno, school year 1935-1936, preserved at MuSEd, Department of Educational Sciences, Roma Tre University*

Pic. 3.13. *Lombardo Radice Educational Archive, MuSEd, Department of Educational Sciences, Roma Tre University, primary school of Sassari, Sardinia, Teacher Olga Raffaelli, school year 1936-1937*

Fig 3.14. Lombardo Radice Educational Archive, MuSEd, Department of Educational Sciences, Roma Tre University, primary school exercise book, school year 1936-1937

Pic. 3.15. *Lombardo Radice Educational Archive, MuSEd, Department of Educational Sciences, Roma Tre University, primary school of Paternò (Catania), school year 1936-1937*

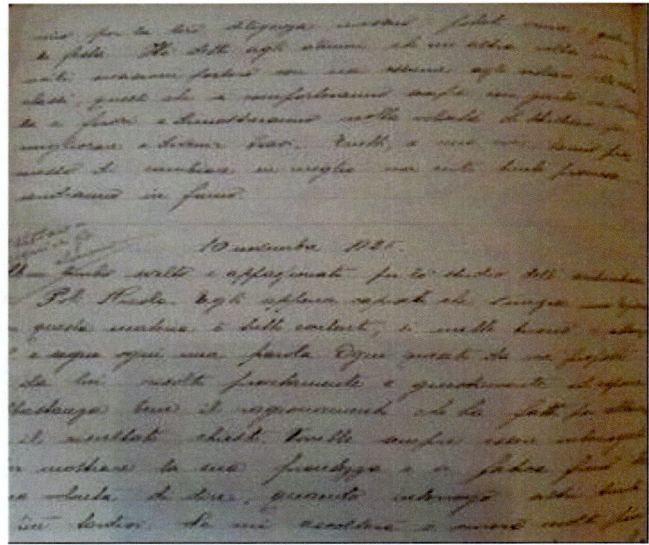

Pic. 3.16. *Lombardo Radice Educational Archive, MuSEd, Department of Educational Sciences, Roma Tre University, a primary school teacher's diary, mixed-class rural school, Morciano di Romagna, school year 1925-1926*

Pic. 3.17. *Lombardo Radice Educational Archive, MuSEd, Department of Educational Sciences, Roma Tre University, primary school of Sassari, Sardinia, Teacher Olga Raffaelli, school year 1936-1937*

Furthermore, in recent years, exercise books have been the subject of historiographical attention in relation to the children's drawings with which they are often richly accompanied, giving rise to new forms of cataloguing archives and increasing its studies in that direction. Perhaps, even more than writing, children's drawings could help scholars not only to investigate this expressive form as a learning tool[50], but also to intercept mentalities, visions of the world, as well as children's experiences, affections, and emotions, which are one of the most innovative frontiers of the new histori-

---

[50] "Experts in Art and Image Education teaching ceased to consider children's drawings as inferior figurative manifestations – characterised by stereotypical contents, essential forms and superficial style – and started a lively debate relating to the recognition of children's artistic graphic expression and the chance of referring to it with the term 'children's art'" (Meda 2007).

ography[51]. From this perspective, the creation of IRAND network[52] (International Archives Network Historical Children's Drawings), which archives children and young people's drawings in the 20th century, is evidence of a growing sensitivity in this sense (Borruso & Cantatore 2021a).

Drawings are part of an international network, which collects, preserves and studies children and young teenagers' drawings, borrowed from both school life and private collections where children's freedom of expression is even more evident.

The cataloguing card created for this purpose is very detailed and is focused both on the valorisation of the techniques used and the identification of the dominant topics. In reality, the valorisation of the children's artistic dimension was not always easy to achieve in school educational practices, especially in rural schools, as it was considered unnecessarily distracting for boys and girls, who would have had to devote themselves to farm- or housework. Nonetheless, some educational experiences, even in rural schools, bear witness to the valorisation of children's drawings, which were sometimes experienced in a spontaneous and freeway and other times with a descriptive or faithfully reproductive function, borrowed from the surrounding reality – as in the case of the famous *Quaderni di San Gersolè* in Maria Maltoni's school – or other

---

[51] For the recent historiographical frontier of the history of emotions, see Boquet & Nagy (2016); at a historical-educational level see Borruso, Cantatore & Covato (2014), and Covato (2018).

[52] The network is a cooperating institution of the Subcommittee on Education and Research (SCEaR), *Memory of the World* UNESCO Programme. The international research and archive network for children and young people's drawings has existed since 2017 and connects archives, collections and research institutes all over the world with the aim of investigating images, which were made by teenagers, <https://international-archives.net/en/home-2/> (12.01.2021).

artistic sources thanks to some enlightened teachers' devotion and in the wake of the educational renewal movements belonging both to new schools, which have been already spreading in Europe since the second half of the nineteenth century, and to pedagogical activism, as well as the idea of a serene school, which was elaborated by Giuseppe Lombardo Radice.

Within the category of exercise books we also want to include school diaries written by teachers. Although these documents, like all the autobiographical documents (Lejeune 1975), are difficult to interpret, they can be valuable for several reasons. Firstly, because they were written by privileged witnesses of the educational relationship; because they are mostly focused on the narration of everyday school life; because they give visibility to obscure teachers from the past, who would otherwise remain completely out of collective memory[53], and because they can be useful in intercepting the relationship between theory and practice within school life, similarly to children's exercise books. Furthermore, they can reveal some information on the training and professionalisation processes of teachers (Brighigni 2010, pp. 175 ff.) and on the self-representation of teaching status, precisely because they are more markedly autobiographical documents, although they were written in the past as a result of an institutional obligation. This information, which changes with the political-cultural and historical-educational context, is valuable for understanding the role and function of teachers in community life (Demetrio 2004).

---

[53] In this regard, I would like to point out the research borrowed from the teachers' direct voice in Paciaroni (2020).

Some proposals for cataloguing exercise books

How to deal with this complex kind of source at an archival level, trying to enhance its multiple implications in scientific research and teaching, which have been briefly reconstructed in this contribution?

In fact, the need to design a cataloguing card based on the specificity of a school exercise book, emerges not only to preserve the integrity of this material document, but also to increase and facilitate those research paths, which are now laboriously pursued through widespread eventful research carried out by each scholar, who cannot currently make use of an *ad hoc* network[54].

Our proposal is also based on the recent experience of the PRIN project of national interest, financed by the Ministry of Research, entitled *School Memories between Social Perception and Collective Representation (Italy, 1861-2001)*[55]. With the participation of several Italian universities[56], the project has created the online database *Memoria scolastica*, which includes a heterogeneous plurality of sources on school history now available in open access. The sources relating to school history in a period between 1861 and 2001 are heterogeneous because they include audio/video, photographic,

---

[54] For this purpose, there are isolated realities, such as the Exercise Book Archive, or disparate and non-homogeneous cataloguing forms, which do not facilitate scholars.

[55] The national project was coordinated by Prof. Roberto Sani (University of Macerata).

[56] Led by the University of Macerata, the PRIN has involved research units at the University of Roma Tre, the Catholic University of the Sacred Heart of Milan, and the University of Florence. Then, there are several aggregated scholars, who come from the Universities of Turin, Bolzano, Genoa, Campobasso, Bologna, Foggia, Padua, Bergamo.

cinematographic, literary, autobiographical, iconographic school memories, as well as medals, decorations, and school awards.

In the wake of this research experience, which gave rise to a deeply innovative pilot project in terms of cataloguing sources and designing/creating an open access database, the cataloguing card of exercise books could be conceived as follows.

Firstly, it should analyse exercise books as physical objects:

1. Photo of the front/back exercise book;

2. Size of the exercise book;

3. Paper used (if identifiable);

4. Type of binding;

5. Type of lining (lines, squares);

6. Iconography of the cover;

7. Seriality of the iconography for the cover and belonging to any styles;

8. Author of the images shown;

9. Condition of the object (if there is any restoration).

Then, the object should be analysed in relation to its contents. Thus, the following items could be contemplated:

10. Place of conservation for the exercise book (archive or collection) and its location;

11. The dating of the exercise book;

12. The village, city, region of origin;

13. The name of its author, or just the sex of its author;

14. The age of its author;

15. The name of the reference teacher;

16. The reference school: name of the school, city, any possible teaching club;

17. School level (primary school, secondary school; school year);

18. Study subject: (Maths, Italian, History, etc.);

19. Any possible notes in the margins (teachers' comments);

20. Any possible drawings in the exercise book. In relation to drawings, the techniques used (tempera, watercolour drawings, etc.) could also be indicated;

21. Brief outline of the contents in the exercise book from which the dominant topics and issues can be highlighted;

22. Teaching methods (if expressly mentioned);

23. Tags: the provision of a number of tags (to be defined), which are focused on the topics and issues emerging from the contents of the exercise book, could be very useful to allow fast and large-scale IT research;

24. The names of historical figures mentioned in the exercise book;

25. The bibliography.

A cataloguing card designed in this way – although it can certainly be perfected and extended in terms of a plurality of levels – is primarily intended to highlight the need for further consideration of some elements (themes, research paths, questions) that can be useful for the improvement of historical-educational research. For example, identifying the school of origin would allow scholars to look for sources, which are focused on a specific area; dating an exercise book would allow to select sources in relation to a specific historical period; identifying the name or sex of its author could facilitate in looking for gender differences in school production and so on. Furthermore, a brief outline could guide the identification of some dominant topics, which would be strengthened by tags. Instead, a question, which would deserve a further deep examination, is the indication relating to teaching methods, since they are not always explicit and so easily able to be intercepted.

We could start from such a cataloguing card, which is completely hypothetical and the result of the historical-educational sensitivity of our study group, in order to deeply examine the debate on cataloguing exercise books in the hope that it will be possible to construct a dedicated card, which takes into account the extraordinary specificity of this source for history of education and is able to be questioned on a multiplicity of interpretative levels.

Chapter 4

Observing and Describing Objects: Cataloguing as a Method for Learning in Schoolwork

Marta Brunelli

Preface

This contribution aims to analyse the educational potential of cataloguing heritage objects in general, and particularly those from school historical heritage, in educational contexts. For this purpose, we will explore the assumptions and methods that enable us to utilise a formal and seemingly unimaginative activity, such as creating a cataloguing description, in an educational context with the precise aim of supporting the educational path and learning objectives of the school.

When we think about cataloguing, all those places and contexts – from libraries to museums, from archives to excavation areas and so on – come to mind. This is because cultural heritage is the object of heritage conservation, study, and valorisation interventions, where cataloguing is a preliminary and necessary phase. It is no coincidence that the Cultural Heritage and Landscape Code (Legislative Decree 42/2004) dedicates a significant portion of Art. 17 to cataloguing (within Title I, which specifically addresses Protection), highlighting it as a fundamental prerequisite for conservation. This emphasises the importance of having precise knowledge and a comprehensive description of the objects we wish to preserve and enhance.

It should also be considered that cataloguing – understood as a systematic collection of standardised data based on specific criteria – is the final step in a series of preparatory activities. This process begins with a research and study phase, which can be carried out at various levels of in-depth examination, with the goal of understanding the specific cultural asset that will be catalogued. In essence, the cultural asset is analysed as a whole, both as a tangible and historical object, and is then situated within a network of relationships with other objects and contexts. This network spans from the cultural context in which it was produced to the current context in which it is read and interpreted.

Therefore, cataloguing is intended as a:

> moment of recognition for such an asset, considering its physical consistency and dual historical value – past and present – and its role in a complex and dynamic process, which spans from knowledge to transmission to the future through the conservation of the Cultural asset, both in its materiality and for the historical memory it represents. From this structure of the Cultural asset – meant as an artefact and historical memory – we derive the theoretical principles of the catalogue, which serve as the foundation for all our registration practices (Vasco Rocca 2003, p. 22).

In addition to being the end point of the – collective and explicit – process to recognise the cultural value, which that object bears, the cataloguing act can be considered as a *cognitive process* to all the intents and purposes as it involves a variety of complex activities whose training potential can be also usefully exploited in the school context to facilitate the acquisition of knowledge and skills relating to different fields of knowledge. Therefore, the specific object of this intervention is to highlight the training potential of these activities for the purposes of its use in the school context and daily teaching.

Working with objects: from exploratory games to goal-directed activities

Maria Montessori stated that there is a sort of "voice of things" with which objects attract the attention of children, especially the youngest ones, and invite them to touch, explore and, finally, "work" with them in some way. The material qualities of an object – from shape to colour, weight and so on – have this intrinsic power to stimulate the multi-sensory and intellectual involvement of children, who observe it. Montessori writes that:

> The teacher supervises, it is true; but there are things of various kinds that attract children of various ages. Brightness, colours, beauty of lively and adorned things are really so many "voices", which attract the children's attention and stimulate them to act. These objects have an eloquence, which no teacher could ever achieve: "take me", they say; "keep me intact, put me in my place." And the action, which is performed in accordance with this invitation, gives children that joyful satisfaction, that awakening of energy, which prepares them for the most difficult tasks of intellectual development. There is a voice of things, which attracts; attraction is a complex order: some important tasks require not only a single child, but an organised

community, with training and long preparation (Montessori 1948/2018, p. 102).

As it is known, in the passage mentioned above, Montessori refers to practical life activities, such as setting the table, serving lunch, and washing the dishes. Children from nursery school love to engage in these activities with a level of concentration that the Italian pedagogist describes as "attention". This concentration is the expression of the children's most powerful creative force and, at the same time, a prefiguration of the intellectual potential of future adults.

In hindsight, the same principle of gradual complexity, which sees children progressively involved in the first simple practical activities up to "important tasks" implying "an internship and a long preparation" – to use Montessori's words – can be traced back in all the laboratory activities, which first the children and then the young people will meet as they progress through their school and, more in general, their educational path. Applying the laboratory method in education means activating ways of knowledge that connect theory with practice, thought with action. This approach promotes autonomy, activism, puerocentrism, which have been the foundation of every pedagogical and didactic innovation for centuries. These principles have consistently originated from the direct manipulation of objects, which then become the focus of a finalised task, starting with creative games.

In this regard, Franca Zuccoli (2010) not only reconstructed the historical stages of pedagogical and psychological research on the pedagogical value of objects, but also outlined the fundamental and recurring principles in the operational proposals developed throughout the history of education, starting from Comenius, through Rousseau or the Froebelian lesson and, naturally, John Dewey's *learning by doing*, up to the most recent experiments, which were developed in Italian and foreign schools in the 2000s. Zuccoli highlights that if the object "already carries a series of meaningful discovery actions, which children naturally create, when they interact with it", all those educational actions planned by adults which transform the learners' initial free discovery into a more articulated and structured learning path, imply a very different complexity of procedures (Zuccoli 2010, p. 105).

To underline the significance of the heuristic and cognitive value of free discovery, Zuccoli recalls research conducted by physicist and educator David Hawkins since the 1960s. Hawkins experimented with new methods of teaching science to primary school children and identified the cognitive and creative importance of what he called "messing about". Messing about refers to those real games of exploration and manipulation of objects and materials, which are carried out by children when they are left free to build and experiment without adult control or instructions. This is a truly "free and unguided" working style, and although it may seem unproductive (chaotic and not finalised), this initial phase of discovery prepares children to embrace the next, more organised and externally directed ways of working, which include: reflection-stimulating questions and instructions guided by teachers, conference-explanation, and class debate aimed at generalizing results (Hawkins 1979, pp. 85-86). However, this is the phase of free practical experimentation, instilling a research-oriented mindset and a way of working that will be fundamental for the future:

> The need to get to know the variety of things and phenomena in a pure and simple way is even more evident here [*i.e.*, in the "messing about" phase], before being able to

embark on some of the paths that lead to great general-
isations […]. With time and a good mix of this phase of
work with other people, the "messing about" evolves and
changes in quality together with children. The kind of
self-disciplined and exploratory investigation that is the
essence of creativity becomes a way of working, which is
no longer childish, even if it always belongs to childhood
(Hawkins 1979, pp. 87-88).

Returning to the phases of observation, interaction and manipulation - which are considered as a specific learning way based on
active work with and on objects – it is worth recalling Montessori's passage on the voice of objects one last time. This is a call
that objects throw to the little ones through their own colour, the
smoothness of a table surface, or the shape of objects, inviting children to take, manipulate and use them, as the Italian pedagogist
explains. In 1979, the psychologist James J. Gibson gave this sort
of "invitation" the name *affordance*, a term he coined to define the
general qualities and properties of an object, which activate the
potential of the actions that people can perform on it: catching,
manipulating, pulling, biting, kicking it and so on (Gibson 1999).

According to Gibson's ecological theory of perception, these properties are the result of the relationship that is naturally and directly
established between the perceived object and the subject who
perceives it in a context. Observing objects involves immediately
activating a process for elaborating the stimuli, which the environment already presents to us, and translating them into action
– even if this action remains merely potential. Today, after the
discovery of mirror neurons by neurosciences, we understand that
there is no clear separation between observation and action. Both
support the processes of understanding and interpreting reality:

"seeing that they guide the hand is also, and above all, seeing *with* the hand, with respect to which the perceived object immediately appears codified as a determined set of action hypotheses". This enables people to orient themselves and, consequently, be ready to move and act in the world around them (Rizzolatti & Sinigaglia 2006, pp. 49-50).

In consideration of these premises, it is evident that the field of education is motivated to cultivate observation and descriptive abilities with regard to both objects and the surrounding reality. It is no coincidence that several Italian and foreign educators dedicated specific operational manuals, particularly designed for first cycle schools. In Italian language, we highlight the texts *Imparare a descrivere* by the teachers and psychologists Ferruccio Bianchi and Patrizia Farello (2010a and 2010b). Here, the authors, after highlighting the importance of *descriptive skills* as a cross-cutting educational objective of the school curriculum, demonstrate how description is a complex mental process involving various sub-processes. Based on this, I am taking the liberty of grouping these sub-processes into two general main phases:

- the initial phase is represented by *direct observation* consisting of an analysis of the object, which is supported by a multisensory exploration aimed at collecting the greatest amount of information available, starting from the use of the privileged sense of sight;

- instead, the next phase of the process corresponds to the reorganization of information for a representative function and involves the mental processes of *comparing, conceptualising* and *defining*; the latter is understood as "that mental operation, which allows the essential representation of reality to be processed by specifying what it is in its dimensions of manner, place, time, cause" (Bianchi & Farello 2010a, pp. 14-15).

The complexity, interdisciplinarity and transversality of these activities, which allow people to mobilise multiple knowledge and skills, are evident: for example, the linguistic skills, which are necessary to verbally describe an object (in written or oral form), without considering the specific technical-lexical knowledge, which is acquired in order to properly describe and define the features of an animal or a plant, a building or a geographical place, etc. Finally, these skills are immediately transferable to the most different situations and contexts: to describe a natural event (e.g., an atmospheric phenomenon), but also a social event (from a family moment to a social situation), to describe a real person as a fictional character or, finally, to recognize and describe an emotion – in fact, Bianchi and Farello propose targeted and differentiated teaching activities for each kind of objects and situations. Consequently, observational skills are developed first and then descriptive ones. This development occurs on both a formal and content-representative level and commences from a common procedural basis. It is posited that such a basis can then be utilised to plan and strengthen further and increasingly elaborate cognitive activities ranging from the interpretation of the real world up to reflection on imaginary or inner worlds.

Describing as a form of knowledge: Pedagogical implications

Following these premises, direct observation and description of objects must be understood not only as the manifestation of a specific way of multisensory and exploratory knowledge, which is privileged in children, but also as the basis of an active, creative, and inclusive pedagogy capable of stimulating multifaceted learning processes.

Object-based teaching is *active* since direct manipulation gives learners the active role of explorers, who are allowed to interact with the world and experience concrete reality first hand, rather than receiving abstract concepts and facts from a theoretical lesson or a textbook. It is *creative* because the implementation of multisensory teaching and learning methods makes it possible to break down the primacy of some senses over others, or of one language over others, in the sense of the Theory of a Hundred Languages by Loris Malaguzzi, the founder of the Reggio Emilia approach. Just to give voice to the multiple ways in which children know, work and enter a relationship with the outside world, Malaguzzi introduced in preschool and primary education the *Creative Atelier*, where all those "other" talents and non-verbal skills, i.e., manual, visual-spatial, musical skills, etc., are valued (Malaguzzi & Gandini 2017). In other words, this approach entails the collapse of the primacy of one "intelligence" over another – considered in the sense of Howard Gardner's Theory of Multiple Intelligences – and questions the primacy of one discipline over another, and more precisely of academic disciplines and skills (i.e. the linguistic-verbal, logical-mathematical ones) over others such as spatial, musical, kinaesthetic, interpersonal, intrapersonal (Gardner 2013). All these approaches have changed the vision of education and learning towards a more inclusive perspective, attentive to the valorisation of individual abilities and inclinations (Gardner 2022).

Based on these premises, it can rightly be said that object-based pedagogy is inclusive, because the multisensoriality implies the valorisation of plural and alternative cognitive methods as well as the promotion of a multimodal, interdisciplinary and global dimension of knowledge.

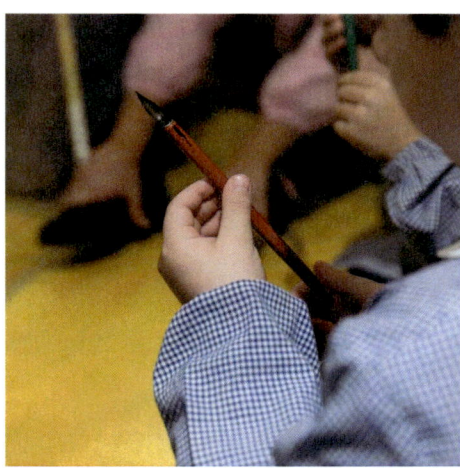

Pic. 4.1. *(on the left) Observing the nib and its parts; wondering how it works; and finally learning the related nomenclature;* **Pic. 4.2**. *(on the right) Impossible not to touch: which material is it made of? (Photo by Lucia Paciaroni © 2017 "Paolo e Ornella Ricca" School Museum)*

Once again, Maria Montessori reminds us that the harmonious development of all the senses, which are applied to the process of knowledge, does nothing other than predispose the individual to a fundamental attitude, which is valid not only for the time in which the pedagogist-doctor wrote, but also for our time.

> By creating *observant people*, the education of the senses performs not only a generic function of adaptation to the current civilization, but it also directly prepares for practical life. […] In practical life, everyone has the fundamental need to accurately collect stimuli from the environment. […] Therefore, the education of the senses should methodically

begin in childhood and then, continue during the period of education, which will have to prepare individuals for practical life in the environment. Otherwise, we isolate people from the environment (Montessori 1948/2018, pp. 170-173).

But what are the skills, which are promoted by the observation of objects?

The activity of observing and describing combines the first practical, manual, and exploratory component, which is linked to the interaction with concrete artefacts, a series of components, which contribute to the acquisition of a more articulated knowledge.

Regardless of various cognitive and emotional implications, which interaction with artefacts entails – particularly if they are historical –, it should be underlined that the operations of describing and cataloguing objects, whether familiar or completely unknown, require the application of specific competencies for each phase into which the observational/descriptive process is divided (Durbin, Morris, & Wilkinson 1990, Lane & Wallace 2011; Bianchi & Farello 2010a and 2010b).

Learning to observe

Visual competencies are not innate, but they require gradual exercise to be especially aimed at a specific purpose. Although sight represents the main sense, which guides our exploration of the world around us through the spontaneous act of "seeing", on the contrary, observational competence needs to be trained to collect, interpret and select information, which is necessary for our purpose.

Considered as a competence to be developed, observation can be facilitated and supported thanks to the use of a series of questions, which adults (educators, teachers, museum operators) propose to students to guide them in the visual and material exploration of each object. The guiding questions do not concern the discovery of the object and its function (*What is it?*), but they rather have the aim at addressing the observer's attention to the investigation of different properties of the object from the most diversified points of view as possible: from physical and material features (*What colour is it? What shape is it? What is it made of? What is its weight? What size is it?*) to the way in which it was made (*Was it produced manually or not? Was it made in a single piece or several parts?*) and the function in relation to the shape and the parts composing it (*How was it used?*) and so on.

Learning to ask questions

As we have seen, the role of the educator is precious in guiding this first approach to observation through the suggestion of stimulating questions, which help young people to gradually approach and assimilate the basic dynamics of this "oriented seeing" to which they are not naturally used.

Pic. 4.3. *Observing a mysterious object. How was it made? What shape is it? What does it look like? How could it be used? (Photo by Marta Brunelli © 2019 "Paolo e Ornella Ricca" School Museum)*

The purpose of these questions is not to obtain a right answer but rather to lead observers to acquire a precise method for observing and investigating reality and its phenomena and acquiring the foundations of what is called Inquiry-Based Learning (IBL), which is also promoted by the European Commission with particular regard to the teaching of scientific subjects, in the form of Inquiry-Based Science Education recommended (Rocard 2007, Scapellato 2017).

From this initial observation – which the teacher will stimulate with guiding questions and will lead through the different phases of the description according to a structured map) – new questions will inevitably arise, some from the pupils themselves. If an answer is not known, this will lead to further discussions and to investigations on the object by the pupils and work groups involved in the description. These questions have been defined by the pedagogist Daniele Novara as maieutic or generative questions:

> Maieutic questions are posed to uncover the unknown, not to test knowledge. This is why they are generative questions, as the term that defines them suggests. They delve into the unknown, seeking to uncover what lies within and beyond us, and what has been hidden from the confines of tradition, custom and stereotype. They offer opportunities to build open and sustainable learning paths. […] Learning is not about finding the right answers, but about applying skills, which means knowing how to use knowledge in a practical, concrete, and real-life context (Novara 2018, pp. 93-94).

Learning to describe involves the acquisition of all the observation and analysis competencies linked to the exploration of the reality surrounding us, learning to master the formulation of appropriate questions, which are functional to the intended purpose. This aspect characterizes the explorers and the researchers' mental *habitus* and, after having been recognized as instinctive in children, it is now increasingly recognized as a potential to be developed in teenagers, who prove to be perfectly able to work in a self-directed way and to manage complex processes to the point that, as Monica Guerra writes, "their spontaneous attitude to investigate, but also their propensity to welcome unexpected outcomes, to revise their ideas and to more easily assume that their knowledge is incomplete and temporary, place them in a more opened position as researchers than adults" (Guerra 2022, p. 44). But what other processes can be unblocked to activate this potential in young researchers?

Learning to formulate hypotheses

Reasoned observation leads to a series of increasingly sophisticated logical operations needed to explain new and unknown objects or to solve problems (*How does it work? What is it for? Who uses it?*). To answer to generative questions, it is necessary to learn to reflect, to discuss with your peers, to formulate one or more theories about the use of an object, to hypothesise its function on the basis of the information we have (e.g., shape, weight, material), to try to reconstruct its features starting from a fragment and so on.

Hypothetical thinking intervenes in this phase and involves the use of all the available data in order to build one or more plausible hypotheses, which are based on evidence and correctly reasoned. Introducing this kind of thinking into educational work involves replacing what Jerome Bruner defines as traditional teaching in an enunciative form with teaching in a hypothetical form:

> In hypothetical teaching, teachers and students are in a more cooperative position [...]. Pupils are not desk-bound listeners, but they can actively take part in expositions and formulations and can sometimes play a leading role. They are aware of some alternatives, towards which they can also take an "as if" attitude and evaluate some information as they receive it. [...] Only the hypothetical form can characterise teaching that encourages discovery (Bruner 2005, p. 109).

Observers, who are motivated by curiosity and guided by questions about the object, proceed on their learning path with the verification of the hypotheses they have just elaborated through simple experimentations, which demonstrate their validity: in this regard, Bruner is always enlightening by introducing us with that way of thinking, which he defines as *paradigmatic* or *logical-scientific thinking* – in a relationship of contrast/complementarity with *narrative thinking* –, operating in a context, which «has not only the observable realities to which his fundamental assertions refer, but also the set of possible worlds, which can be logically produced and compared with observable realities; and this is because paradigmatic thinking is guided by hypotheses based on principles» (*ibidem*). Once again, activities, such as observation, analysis and (verbal or visual) representation of objects, prove to be functional in the acquisition of skills and competences belonging to scientific thinking.

Learning to represent

The graphic representation of the observed object is complementary – but also functional in some way – to the act of describing, for example, through drawing, which involves and entertains not only students of all ages, but it is a real tool of knowledge, which is able to develop further observation competences and to activate "other" methods of data collection, selection and reprocessing. Here, we cannot fail to recall the importance of mobilising all the Gardnerian intelligences, including the visuo-spatial one, in an integrated form, as Gardner writes:

> the abilities to perceive the visual world with precision, to carry out changes and modifications of one's first perceptions and to be able to recreate aspects of one's visual experience play a central role in spatial intelligence (Gardner 2013, p. 254).

As it can be seen from the picture, which is shown here (Pic. 4.4), drawing is not just a mere reproductive activity, but it can become a cognitive activity when it is used by observers to collect, select and carefully re-elaborate both global and detailed data. Proposing to draw objects from different and unusual angles represents a challenge of creativity, which will push students to explore reality from various perspectives, choosing new points of view, which are able to offer new data or other kinds of information.

Creating a representation of the observed objects through a graphic work – be it a drawing or a photo, a collage, a video recording, etc. – does not prefigure only one of the essential phases for describing and cataloguing activities, which are always completed by an iconographic set in professional practice. On the one hand, creating a graphic work is actually also configured as a functional activity to increasingly discover and record new complex information, data and details, which can enrich our knowledge of the observed objects; on the other hand, it is a re-elaborating exercise for reality, which is able to stimulate the fancy and creativity of the pupils, who are pushed to explore real forms of artistic expression – when they are invited to (re)construct their own personal vision of the external world –, as demonstrated by the analogies between the drawing, which was made by a primary school child to document his research on the objects in his classroom (Pic. 4.4) and some works by contemporary artists (Pic. 4.5).

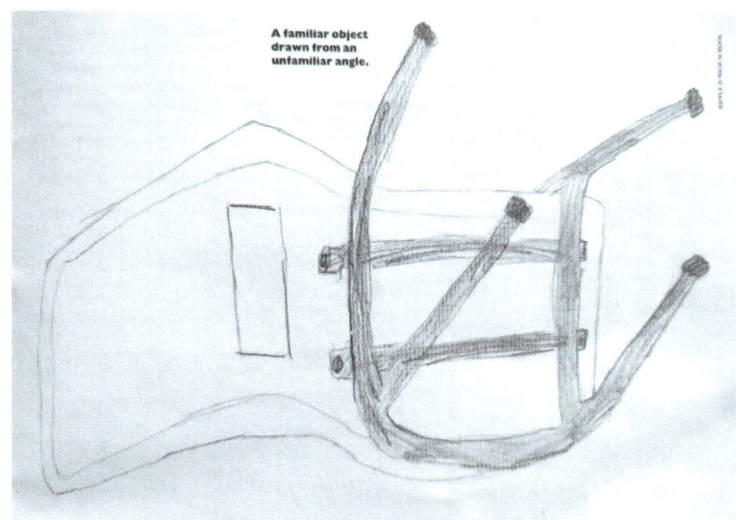

Pic. 4.4. *A familiar object, which is observed from an unusual perspective (source: Durbin, Morris, & Wilkinson 1990, p. 21)*

Pic. 4.5. *Michael H. Rodhe, Own kitchen, photo (2010), (source: <https://www.michael-h-rohde.de/>. This reproduction has been kindly authorised by the Author*

Learning to classify

Another fundamental aspect of the description is classification, which implies the abstract conceptualization of the features and properties in the objects observed (e.g., material, colour, shape, structure, function). Through the reorganization of the data provided by experience – and a process of abstraction –, the observed qualities and properties are translated into categories thanks to which observers learn to compare, identify analogies and differences and, finally, classify objects according to precise criteria. Learning to classify (another fundamental element for the description) means using conceptual thinking as a powerful tool for understanding objects and their function and meaning. Once again, this activity brings us to the research method and the domain of what Bruner defined as paradigmatic thinking, that is, thinking, which "resorts to categorization or conceptualization, as well as the operations through which categories are constituted, elevated to symbols, idealised and put in relation to each other so as to create a system" (Bruner 1988, p. 19).

Learning to catalogue

Cataloguing is the synthesis of all the previous activities.

Cataloguing is nothing other than the systematization of all the information, which is collected up to that moment – be they *primary data,* because they are obtained from direct observation of objects and their qualities, or *secondary data,* because they are reconstructed with the support of external sources or integrated with plausible hypotheses – and its recording using a variety of tools.

Cataloguing represents the common thread and the final objective of educational projects, which can be differently constructed, but they can be directly linked to the learning objectives of any discipline in the curriculum, whether it is the drafting of an inventory list (which is concise, but functional for future activities), the drafting of (more or less analytical) descriptive cards to be included in a paper (or digital/virtual) catalogue, the creation of captions or information panels, which are functional to the preparation of an exhibition, or even the creation of a deeply examined historical dossier, which is aimed at illustrating the history of the objects or the materials examined.

For this reason, the term *pedagogical cataloguing* – coined by Francesca Pizzigoni[57] – has been adopted here to mean an organised learning-focused description of artefacts. This cataloguing, even if broadly based on the general principles of scientific cataloguing for cultural heritage, once transferred to the school environment, transforms into the teaching and learning strategy known as Authentic Learning (Lombardi 2007). Cataloguing school artefacts becomes an authentic task because it is an exercise related to the real life:

- it relates to students' daily experiences and, potentially, interests and needs;

- it simulates open but realistic problems that are relevant to the professional world (e.g. of museums);

- it engages students by calling them to harness resources and make choices to solve problems in the specific context;

---

[57] See *below*, the paragraph 1 of the chapter *Pedagogical Cataloguing: Proposing Initial Cataloguing Activities linked to School Activities* in this volume

- it involves small group working methods;

- it requires the application of existing knowledge as well as the development of new multidisciplinary competencies. Let's just think about the lexical mastery needed to properly describe an object, as well as the specialist disciplinary knowledge necessary to understand its function and illustrate its use.

As we can see, the educational potential of pedagogical cataloguing is vast.

Describing the heritage in the classroom as a teaching strategy

If the description of a common object involves the development of many different cognitive activities, which have been examined above, the description of an object from the past is even more complex, whether it is an "old" family object (full of memories, stories and personal or family meanings) or an object, which has already been in a museum and recognized as the bearer of various complex historical and cultural messages.

In fact, the observation of ancient objects, which are often obsolete and, therefore, difficult to be interpreted by modern observers, must necessarily be completed by information obtained from external sources, which are different from each other and able to integrate and complete each other: just think about heritage inventories and archival materials, which testify to the creation of a museum collection, or historical sources and testimonies – handed down from autobiographies, literary texts, oral sources, etc. – which describe how those objects were produced or used in daily life.

Thus, cataloguing becomes an extremely complex cognitive activity during which not only observation, lexical and descriptive competences, but also competences of historical research and competent use of sources, which are functional to collecting the necessary data for the recognition and the cultural and historical recontextualization of that object, are mobilised – especially in the case of an ancient, obsolete or unknown object. These last competences are not acquired with theoretical study, but only through direct application to an authentic task: the one represented by the study of original objects.

The educational implications of the interaction with historical artefacts have been widely explored especially in Anglo-Saxon literature, both in school and museum contexts and, more recently, also in higher education. Since 1990, teaching practices based on direct observation and description of real objects have been adopted in British schools (Durbin, Morris, & Wilkinson 1990, Lane & Wallace 2011). In the same period, significant attention was given to the educational potential of the museum environment, particularly museum objects, which are no longer seen solely as an expression of the dominant culture represented by a museum. Instead, they are seen as bearers of messages and multi-vocal interpretations, resulting from an uninterrupted activity of (re)meaning, built through interaction with each individual visitor each time. Various experts have paid attention to learning processes in the museum context, embodying a real *educational turn* which took place in the transition from twentieth to twenty-first century museology. Among them we can mention the sociologist of education Eilean Hooper Greenhill (1992 and 1999), but also psychologists and pedagogists, such as Scott Paris (Paris 2002), Gaea Lein-hardt (Leinhardt & Crowley 2002) and Lynn Dierking (Dierking 2002), the biologist Helen Chatterjee (Chatterjee 2008, Chatterjee & Hannan 2015)[58], or anthropologists like Sandra Dudley (2012 and 2010). These scholars have all put forward theoretical proposals and tested teaching practices that confirmed the catalytic power historical artefacts exert in the experience of the visitors, where these are left free to explore, interpret and actively carry out their own learning experience.

In particular the research group at the University College of London led by Chatterjee definitely coined the expression OBL-*Object-Based Learning* to indicate an educational approach, which reintroduced the use of artefacts coming from university museum collections into the university study (Pic. 4.6), renewing and adapting it to the twenty-first-century training needs: for example, by linking it to the acquisition of digital competences (Tiballi 2015).

---

[58] Further information on the project can be found in the URL: <https://www.ucl.ac.uk/culture/schools/teaching-object-based-learning> (12.12.2021).

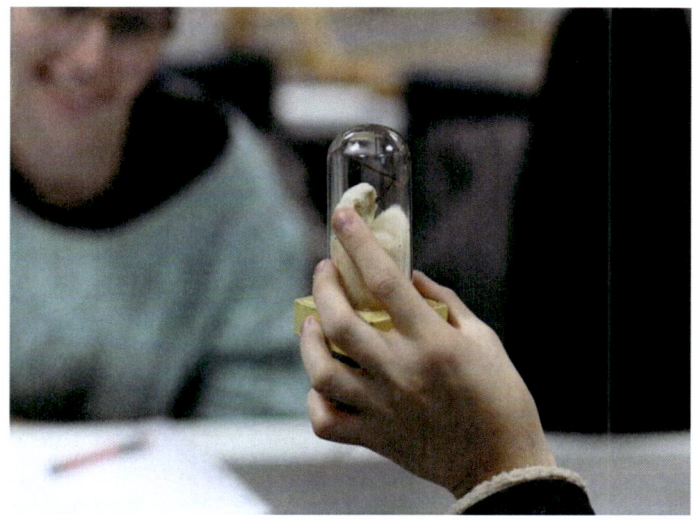

Pic. 4.6. *Object-Based Learning sessions, which are based on the study of samples from the naturalistic collections at the University College of London. Source: Object Based Learning Laboratory, <https://www.ucl.ac.uk/culture/teaching-object-based-learning/student-experience> (10.12.2021)*

Thus, OBL is configured as an active (student-centred) and experiential (activity based learning) didactic approach, which is based on the fact that university students directly use museum artefacts as objects of research and, at the same time, as catalysts for acquiring multidisciplinary knowledge and competences (from natural sciences to civil engineering, from earth sciences to chemistry, from archaeology to museology) and transversal knowledge and competences, such as observation, analysis, identification, communication and teamwork skills, practical skills (measurement, manipulation, etc.), drawing, writing, research and planning (Chatterjee, Hannan, & Thomson 2015).

Proposing works, which are focused on ancient historical artefacts, in a classroom means actively involving students in diversified and complementary activities whose final product may consist, for example:

- in the drafting of (more or less analytical) descriptive cards relating to objects, which are specifically selected for the creation of an educational project or a virtual catalogue, etc.[59];

- in the revision and updating of the old descriptive apparatus of an already existing museum[60];

- finally, in the new creation of descriptive apparatus for a collection of objects according to their preparation for a temporary exhibition inside the school or the museum.

Conceiving, designing and implementing a thematic exhibition or a small museum – even a virtual one – is the end point of various educational projects in schools, whether it is a collection of drawings, dioramas, display boards, photographs or other works, which are produced by students, or the preparation of a thematic itinerary, which is aimed at illustrating the history or meaning of objects, documents and materials, which are specifically collected from the area, the families, the surrounding environment, etc. The creation of an exhibition, which is carried out and introduced by students to the public, represents the ideal result of training courses in schools of all levels since they can have not only any

---

[59] As in the case of NEMO project about which you can see paragraph 2.4 of the essay *Educational cataloguing: proposing initial cataloguing activities linked to school activities* can be seen better *below* in this volume.

[60] Review and update activities for the descriptions of historical artefacts, which were transferred from Petrie Museum at the University College of London to the new *Object-Based Learning Lab*, were carried out online by university students under the supervision of the museum staff during the closing months due to the 2020 *lockdown*. See Garnett (2010).

discipline or topic (from local history to renewable energy) as their object, but they can introduce differentiated levels of complexity to the point of requiring the collaboration of technicians and specialists from local museums[61].

Once again, these processes start from objects before knowledge: *objects* – documents, samples, various materials, which are functional to the exhibition idea and the message to be communicated, – will have to be identified, chosen, described and placed in an intuitive and coherent path.

As the teacher and museum educator Linda D'Acquisto wrote in her handbook specifically dedicated to the creation of exhibitions and museums in schools, the main objective of these projects is not to impart museological skills to students, but to promote an active, stimulating and innovative learning path that is able to:

1) combine the study of curricular subjects (*academic learning*) with the ability to develop creative ideas and implement them (*creative learning*);

2) connect school and community, who is seen as a resource (e.g., archives, libraries, museums and territory) and a recipient of the exhibition;

3) involve students in a complex, stimulating and significant learning path, which is oriented towards the concrete

---

[61] For example, please see the case of the historical-naturalistic museum, which the primary school children at the «Tricase Via Apulia» State Comprehensive Institute in Tricase (LE) created with the consultancy of the Botanical Garden at the University of Salento (Accogli, Nuzzo, & Marchiori 2013).

objective of creating an exhibition or a museum on any disciplinary topic (D'Acquisto 2006 and 2013).

Once entrusted with the responsibility of a museum project (the *student-created museum*), students learn to manage their own learning and to plan their work, to work in groups, to communicate in written and oral forms: in short, they will develop what the European Parliament and Council indicated to the educational policy makers of European countries as the «key competences for lifelong learning», which are indispensable for every citizen (European Commission 2018).

From this perspective, cataloguing clearly emerges no longer just as a technical, extremely formal and highly specialised activity (as it is in the contexts of museums, libraries or archives), but rather as a pedagogical activity, a learning tool and a way of constructing and appropriating knowledge.

In the light of the previous considerations, the great educational potential that educational heritage kept in many Italian schools can still express today, will be even more evident.

All the activities described above, including direct observation and/or manipulation, narrative verbal description, or systematic description organised according to standardised criteria, will be easier to carry out and manage when the school has full access to the cultural heritage. It is clear that teachers and students will be able to plan and implement all the recovery, analysis, comparison, description and classification operations, as outlined above, with greater ease if schools still have a limited number of ancient or simply obsolete objects. Thus, from the observation of an old teaching aid, found in a locker or an obsolete piece of furniture, abandoned in a storeroom, various complex investigation processes can arise, involving students and teachers in an interdisciplinary and coherent project, aimed at setting up a small "room of the school past".

Imagine the research questions that arise from observing an old typewriter, now unused and whose functioning is a mystery to be discovered by today's young people. 'How is it made?' and, above all, 'How does it work?' were the questions that young visitors, from primary school students to high school teenagers, posed when we invited them to discover and experience firsthand some old technologies for writing, including some typewriters, during an interactive exhibition we set up in 2018 (Pic. 4.7).

During the experiential session, the children were given the freedom to explore these unfamiliar objects, which they had never seen before and whose intuitive use was not so easy in practice. The activity we designed as educators (whose role was to engage with visitors, but never to provide them with any instructions or solutions), was precisely to get young people to work out how to do some simple tasks. These tasks included: inserting a sheet of paper into the typewriter, starting a new paragraph, writing in capital letters, or even, erasing a typing error, and even the unexpected use of carbon paper to create a copy of the document. Uncovering the inner workings of these machines – now completely replaced by laptops, handheld computers and printers – required a meticulous process of analysis, exploration, and direct experimentation. Throughout these phases, the boys and girls observed and assisted each other, offering suggestions and taking turns at the mechanical typewriters until they discovered certain functions that were previously unknown to them.

Pic. 4.7. *Interactive exhibition "Science in your pocket. For a history of writing". Exhibition and interpretive script by Marta Brunelli for FermHaMente-Science Festival in Fermo, 2nd Edition (Fermo, 26-28 October 2018). (Ph.: Lucia Paciaroni © 2018 "Paolo e Ornella Ricca" School Museum of Macerata).*

This work can also be done in the classroom and planned as part of an educational project, which aims to create a small historical exhibition on ancient and old school objects. The active phase, when objects are observed and experimented with, will turn the following description activity into a process of meaningful learning.

Let us consider the critical observation based on the comparison between obsolete tools and their modern version, which can be carried out precisely in the school context. Here, recovering the teaching equipment from the past is very easy, and it allows for a comparison with its contemporary counterpart. For example, an old overhead projector and a modern interactive whiteboard (Figg. 4.8-9). Exploring and identifying differences (e.g. in components, construction materials and technologies used) and similarities (in

function and educational purposes), as well as rediscovering operations and usage methods, is of utmost importance in facilitating
the process of understanding and describing objects. Ultimately,
this leads to the acquisition of deeper knowledge, critical thinking
and inquiry as a habit of the mind.

Pics. 4.8-9. *Obsolete and modern teaching aids in comparison: an overhead projector from the 1970s-1980s (source: Piotrus, CC BY-SA 3.0, Wikimedia Commons), and an interactive whiteboard (source: By Lft LFT, CC BY-SA 3.0, Wikimedia Commons).*

These practices could also be included in a broader educational
project, which will be aimed at also creating a small temporary
exhibition of school materials from the school of the past among
various final works. As demonstrated by various experiences,
which were carried out in Italy, this kind of project can become
an interdisciplinary educational project, which is able to involve
students from multiple classes and to be proposed every school
year again, with the aim of giving life to an increasingly rich prepa-

ration, which is likely to become permanent: be it a small room of memories[62] or a real school museum[63].

Where school has particularly precious historical-cultural objects, endless chances for educational valorisation will open up: school artefacts could become the focus of specific educational projects for the valorisation and communication of cultural heritage through the creation of exhibitions open to the public, the promotion of conferences, the publication of studies or catalogues.

The school's historical heritage perfectly exemplifies the "heritage of proximity", which was defined as

> the collection of tangible and intangible cultural heritage components, typically undervalued when viewed solely from an economic perspective, and thus inherently fragile. It can be a building, a tradition, a specific agricultural or artisanal production, or a small village. The fragility of these local components lies in the potential for them to be abandoned, leaving them unable to be passed on to future generations (Buratti & Ferrari 2011, p. 9).

Working on school heritage means recovering and saving from certain dispersion a heritage, which is still often considered invaluable today and, therefore, potentially still fragile but, at the same

---

[62] It is enough to mention the case of «Tommasina Giuliani» Room of the Memories at the primary school of Casalecchio di Reno (BO) or the museum-hall at Edmondo De Amicis primary school museum in Bologna, which were both created with Mirella D'Ascenzo's scientific assistance from the University of Bologna (in particular, for "Tommasina Giuliani" Room of the Memories project, see D'Ascenzo (2019).

[63] See the project *Vuoi costruire il tuo museo scolastico illustrato*, in the paragraph 2.2 of the essay *Educational cataloguing: proposing initial cataloguing activities linked to school activities* in this volume.

time, it means having access to objects with great didactic potential to be used in daily work in the classroom for strengthening interdisciplinary knowledge and competences as well as creating complex curricular projects, such as the creation of an exhibition or a museum on their own school: these projects have proven to be able to enhance the history of a school community and all the other social groups (students' families, neighbourhood or inhabitants of the municipal area, etc.), who have always had an indisputable driving force at school on which the identity of old and new communities is shaped[64].

---

[64] As in the case of the experience for the network of school museums in Turin, see *below* paragraph 2.2 of the essay *Educational cataloguing: proposing initial cataloguing activities linked to school activities* in this volume.

Chapter 5

Pedagogical Cataloguing: Proposing Initial Cataloguing Activities linked to School Activities[65]

Francesca Davida Pizzigoni & Marta Brunelli

Preface: Pedagogical cataloguing

The term "pedagogical cataloguing" does not actually exist. However, there is not even a formula or a way of satisfying the need to indicate what we consider to be a fundamental aspect, that is, the action of bringing students significantly closer to the materials that are part of historical school heritage. In fact, through careful and dedicated study, manipulation, observation and direct contact, a fundamental change takes place. The student moves from being a simple user of heritage or a distracted observer to becoming an active interpreter and protagonist of knowledge. It is a clear change of position and role. Students become full protagonists and take on the role of co-creators of knowledge. Even though they do not have an exhaustive preliminary knowledge of each material with which they come into contact at this stage, their specific

---

[65] This essay is the result of collaboration between the two authors. However, we would like to specify that: Francesca Davida Pizzigoni is the author of paragraphs 1. *Preface*, 2. *Cataloguing experiences at school: state of art*, 2.1 *La Scuola è il nostro Patrimonio*; 2.2 *The Turin school museum network*; 3.3. *Il Patrimoniere*; Marta Brunelli is the author of paragraphs: 2.4. *NEMO project of the Neapolitan Historical Schools* and 3. *Conclusions*.

gaze and particular curiosity allow us to start a process of initial knowledge of the object. With appropriate guidance, students can then observe elements that provide useful details in the process of identifying and interpreting the object, reaching a good level of in-depth study along a path where students move forward to overcome the limits of their initial knowledge. Repeated on different materials, this action not only creates a habit of mind capable of asking questions and seeking answers but also triggers a self-perception of an active and participatory role in their relationship with the school's historical heritage.

Thus, as it can be clearly seen, "pedagogical cataloguing" means an activity that is very far from the properly regulated scientific cataloguing that we are used to talking about – and the discussion of which is referred to in the essay by Mara Orlando and Valeria Viola in this volume. It rather represents a process based on a laboratory action that creates a direct relationship between students and school heritage. The aim is to make the students the protagonists, or rather to create the conditions in which the students feel a *commitment* to the historical-educational heritage: they feel a bond, a spontaneous desire for knowledge, a satisfaction in discovering and interpreting the historical-educational heritage. Thanks to the pedagogical cataloguing, we want to provide students with the tools to "question" historical teaching objects and materials and, thus, to develop competences to act actively towards the historical educational heritage. The theoretical references of this approach can be found in this volume, in Marta Brunelli's essay entitled *Observing and describing objects. Cataloguing as a Method for Learning in Schoolwork.*

In the light of the characteristics and aims of pedagogical cataloguing, it is evident that it does not pretend to be scientific (although it remains rigorous in the information it brings to light) or to compete in any way with "real" cataloguing, but rather to place itself at a different level. Likewise, it seems clear – although it is appropriate to specify it – that such an action requires a phase of support for the students, in order to refine the information, to help them in the process of negotiating meanings, understanding connections and relationships, and seeking new knowledge.

Just as there is no formal definition of "pedagogical cataloguing", there are no standardised tools for carrying it out. In this sense, some worksheets used in the first experiences of educational activities will be presented in the following paragraphs. They can be adapted from time to time according to the age group with which the activity is carried out, the context, the level of in-depth analysis that we want to achieve, as well as the specific type of historical-educational heritage that we wish to work with.

Cataloguing experiences at school: State of the art

The following paragraphs will illustrate some experiences of pedagogical cataloguing that have been started in Italy and that are significant points of reference for those who wish to approach this kind of work.

We would like to underline that the activities described are the result of work carried out by students who, under the guidance of attentive and innovative teachers (and with the help of professionals from the cultural and museum world), have taken direct action on historical artefacts in schools.

"La Scuola è il nostro Patrimonio" (School is Our Heritage)

In the 2000s, the Culture Department of the Municipality of Turin began to develop an in-depth reflection on school heritage. This reflection was based on the principles that had led to the creation of the Urban Ecomuseums in the city a few years earlier. Especially crucial in this process was the direct exchange between the then Director of the City's Department of Culture, Daniele Lupo Jalla, and the famous museologist Hugues de Varine, who had coined the term "ecomuseum" in 1971 and promoted the new vision of heritage in which all the tangible and intangible cultural assets of a community are fully recognised[66]. On that occasion, it was natural to observe that "few places are as shared as schools" (Jalla 2009) and that if everything in which a community recognises itself, its history and its values is part of a heritage, then *the school is* certainly *a heritage*.

Therefore, contrary to what would have been done in a more traditional vision of heritage protection and valorisation activities, the City of Turin has launched a support action for schools. In other words, rather than centralising these actions or gathering this heritage in a single central place, so that the school communities can become aware connoisseurs and promoters of their own heritage, keeping their assets in place.

---

[66] The theory and practice of an ecomuseum emerged within the French *Nouvelle Muséologie* movement between the mid-1960s and the early 1970s, in particular under the influence of the ethnologist and museologist George Henry Rivière's and his young colleague Hugues De Varine, who systematised an innovative way of intending cultural heritage whose boundaries expanded to grasp all the expressions and testimonies of human culture and the concepts of territory and identity (Cancellotti 2011). See De Varine (2005a).

This is a culturally significant choice, which embodies a series of meanings and entails various objectives. It ranges from promoting widespread active citizenship to redefining the role of the school and its relationship with city institutions, framed in terms of co-responsibility and subsidiarity. But this innovative choice also touches on another specific area of reflection: the desire that the study and valorisation of the "new" heritage that the schools were discovering should be carried out with the direct participation of the students. In other words, it had an educational purpose.

This perspective suggested that working with school heritage should be seen as a curricular component, and not an extraneous addition to the "program" or *something more*. It would simultaneously broaden students' knowledge in two distinct areas: school history, which involves understanding the evolution of educational history through its materiality, and heritage, not in an abstract sense, but through active practice. Jalla referred to this as *museum making*, which involves training students to become creators of a museum, specifically a school museum, rather than merely preparing them to be museum visitors. The Turin project aimed to engage students directly involved in a "complex series of operations, leading to the identification, analysis, classification, recording, ordering, introduction, spatial arrangement, and accompaniment of objects and finds with captions and other communication devices" (*ibid.*). In short, students fully become protagonists and experts.

The project, which intended to concretely apply this vision, integrates in this context: *La Scuola è il nostro Patrimonio/L'École est notre Patrimoine* is the European Comenius Regio project, which was developed jointly by the City of Turin and the City of Lyon between 2009 and 2011 to experiment the students' direct work on school heritage[67], also in a cross-vision of points of view between France and Italy. The experimentation was carried out with students of different school levels: primary, lower secondary and upper secondary schools. The publication, which was born from the project (Jalla, Lonjon, Pizzigoni, & Vuillet 2011), certainly represents the report of this experience, but it also intends to be a small manual for teachers, a sort of methodological and didactic guideline for working with the class on the heritage of their own school. The manual offers some significant principles concerning the vision and concept of students' work with school heritage or, if we want to put it in other words, "pedagogical cataloguing", where cataloguing does not mean compliance with cataloguing criteria and the science behind it, but rather arranges the students' cognitive and interpretative approach to school heritage[68], as mentioned in the preface.

The first of these key principles about how students were intended to work with heritage concerns the need to "catalogue" and, namely, to also know the school building. Therefore, they have to be able to recognize it as an element of school heritage and not just a container of school life or other school historical cultural assets. It is not just a matter of understanding the architectural style of the building, but rather questioning and identifying it by searching for elements, such as date of construction, original project,

---

[67] The Italian project partners were the City of Turin, Comitato Italia 150, Fondazione per il Libro, la Musica e la Cultura, the Tancredi Foundation in Barolo, which were coordinated by who is writing, on behalf of the Central Direction for Culture and Education-Museums and Cultural Heritage Service of the City of Turin.

[68] Although referring to students included in specific training courses on cataloguing and, therefore, in the context of professional training, the following essay about the distance between cataloguing theory and practice is very interesting (Galeffi & Sardo 2021).

extensions and renovations, and broadening the analysis to know the social, economic and historical context of which it is a mirror. From a historical-heritage perspective, school buildings can be catalogued using a more technical methodology, as in MIBACT (2009) and Taillefait (2002). On the other hand, Bassil, Crevier, & Lachapelle (2005) present a study that supports the re-evaluation of school buildings as cultural heritage. In this regard, a school building can be catalogued also in an *expressive* and comprehensive manner, revealing the need it addressed at the time of its creation, the pedagogy it referenced, the hygienic-healthcare needs it met, or even the teaching practices it embodied, in addition to architectural-structural data. Therefore, students can report courtyards, canteens, gyms, staff rooms, decorations, special materials, plaques, monumental staircases, banisters, reliefs and so on in their card, which was devoted to the building. And for each element, they can question by starting a real research in class, which can be appropriately supported by the teacher to create their own exhaustive cataloguing card of the school building.

Pic. 5.3 *(on the left) Historical image of Baricco primary school in Turin, which is taken from the website Museotorino.it*

The second principle in the pedagogical cataloguing experience of *La Scuola è il nostro Patrimonio*, concerns the belief that students cannot appropriately catalogue an object relating to school heritage if they have no way of placing it within the historical educational context to which the object refers. Therefore, the approach to this "pedagogical cataloguing" also goes so far as to suggest a discussion of elements of school legislation history and the historical development of the concept of school in its various dimensions. In this case, the direct result will not be the cataloguing card of the single object, but the development of preliminary knowledge and competence in the students, "cataloguers of school heritage", who will be then able to better identify, understand and describe the object thanks to the fact of being able to refer it to the school historical context it expresses in some way.

Given the impossibility of delving into the history of education with students, the indication goes in the direction of providing some contextual elements that help us understand the evolution of the school system as a whole. This includes compulsoriness, mandatory subjects and teaching methods, school timetables, regulations on furniture, rooms and teaching aids in different historical periods.

Pic. 5.4. *The Patrimonieri of the "Rayneri" primary school in Turin analyse a historical educational object found in their school, which still bears the original label from the Institute's late nineteenth-century school museum*

In this way, it is a question of allowing students to feel fully immersed in the reality they are studying: their direct relationship is with the single object they catalogue, but the latter is actually part of a broader set of meanings. Consequently, the role and use of a specific object can be better understood if it is included within a more complete system of elements, which allows us to get to know it. On the other hand, as anticipated, the action of "pedagogical cataloguing" is intended not only as a mere inventory/cataloguing action, but as an activity of training students, growing their knowledge and, at the same time, their competence (being able to link a part with the whole, to manage and correlate information, finding connections etc.). Therefore, in order to carry out this part of work with the heritage, the project *La scuola è il nostro Patrimonio* suggested which basic contextual information can help students to orient within the macro topic "history of education" through a small chart:

– framework laws and school programs for a given period;

– priority objectives of these laws;

– number of students at the time of the main framework laws;

– number of inhabitants at the time of the main framework laws.

This short list shows that the activity was not intended as an end in itself. Rather, it was contextualised within the development of the national school system. It was also linked to demographic data, comparing the number of inhabitants and the number of pupils, in order to highlight the relationship between school and territory and the school's impact on different historical periods.

The third principle, which is expressed in *La scuola è il nostro Patri-monio* related to the topic of "pedagogical cataloguing", is partly connected with the vision, which has been already stated in the previous paragraph, that is, not only considering the single object, but being able to correlate it, thus making a network of meanings emerge whose entire heuristic power exceeds the single one. Here is therefore how the indication had to include the action of cata-loguing a single object within a broader project of knowing school heritage and, specifically, creating a school museum. The action of the project, which is called «Making a museum», provides for the students' direct involvement in every phase.

In this way, very important actions are carried out:

- the knowledge of a very significant reality, such as a *school museum*[69], in the context of school history;

- an expert connoisseur, who can contextualise and relate each asset of a heritage[70];

- a long-term valorisation of the cataloguing work, which is then included into a broader context of creating a school museum where the concrete effects of the students' work are therefore visible;

- students are offered the opportunity to experience how

---

[69] For the history and development of school museums see Brunelli (2020) and chapter 2 in Pizzigoni (2022a).

[70] In this regard see Brunelli (2014). With respect to the need to work in the classroom with cultural heritage in order to create a dialogue among dif-ferent disciplines thanks to the *medium* of heritage, please see the manual *Patrimonio culturale in classe*, result of the three-year European project *HER-EDUC-HERitage EDUCation*, which involved France, Germany, Holland and Italy, available online: <https://www.storiairreer.it/sites/default/files/norme/2005%20Hereduc%20manuale.pdf> (24.11.2021).

a museum is created (thereby, developing competences related to education to heritage and active citizenship);

– a broad impact is obtained from the project, which is able to provide schools with a new multifaceted teaching tool, such as a school museum.

"With the expression *making a museum*, we intended to define the set of practices for identifying, classifying and documenting a – tangible or intangible – asset, which are intended to ensure its conservation, exhibition and communication as a *heritage object*" (Jalla, Lonjon, Pizzigoni, & Vuillet 2011, p. 46).

The sentence fully explains the breadth of the action where students are personally involved. The manual guides to macro-actions and various steps of "making a museum", from the creation of the work team to the identification of the places, from the preliminary planning for the identity and mission of the future museum up to the exhibition and communication phase (Jalla, Lonjon, Pizzigoni, & Vuillet 2011, pp. 43-49). But what is important to underline are the methodological indications included under the word "identifying", which actually express very well what we mean by the term "pedagogical cataloguing", that is, not a scientific and technical cataloguing – for which students would not have the necessary competences –, but a real process of deeply knowing the objects, which are being catalogued, a plural and progressive action, which allows us to "take possession" of assets, to enter into a relationship with them, to thoroughly question them to understand them to our fullest potential, as mentioned. To this aim, the *Twelve commandments of identification* have been defined (Jalla, Lonjon, Pizzigoni, & Vuillet 2011, p. 63).

The twelve commandments of identification[71]

1. Denominating

Each thing corresponds to one or more names: a denomination, but also a word in current use, a technical term. Giving a name to the thing, looking for the ways through which it is called is the first step to identify it.

2. Observing/describing

Observing a thing means identifying its evident or hidden features and qualities in order to describe it, searching for the right words in current vocabularies and/or specialised lexicons to highlight its shape, dimensions, material, technique and period of production, function, etc.

3. Representing

To describe a thing, we can use words, but also images: photography, drawing, technical drawing, filming, which also help us to know, better understand and visually communicate it as well as through writing.

4. Analysing

By observing, describing and depicting a thing, a detailed analysis completes its understanding. The knowledge of non-visible elements is also part of the analysis, using techniques and tools to highlight how much of it is not accessible through the senses.

5. Investigating

71

Investigating means trying to reconstruct the 'biography' of an object, using all useful sources to identify its period of conception, creation, and use, as well as its tangible and intangible changes over time. It also involves collecting information on the people who were engaged in its various phases.

6. Comparing/classifying

The proceeding of the analysis and study of a thing makes use of its comparison with other similar or different things, also leading to its classification within the universe of things. This process leads to the identification of classes, typologies, categories within which things are ordered.

7. Evaluating

Evaluating means assigning a value to things according to criteria and parameters, which depend on objectives and lead to identify its symbolic value, in addition to the use and exchange value of the thing.

8. Ordering/Classifying

Classifying means distinguishing and grouping things according to a logic, a mental order from which a physical order may or may not also derive. Every order is legitimate and everything can be simultaneously ordered in different ways.

9. Inventorying

Inventorying consists of recording each thing, which is collected and stored in a given place or belongs to a given person or body, especially to determine its value. The inventory has a patrimonial function, but also a security one – if it is accompanied by images.

10. Cataloguing

In a museum, cataloguing has a scientific purpose and corresponds to drawing up a card, which collects all the data and information on an asset, accompanying them with notes and devices on the sources used. The catalogue of a museum changes the summary of the cataloguing carried out into a publication.

11. Documenting

The documentation activity includes the collection of all the elements (documents, publications, images, research, analysis, etc.) referring to each asset or a set of them to be preserved and made available to all the people, who are interested in deeply examining their knowledge.

12. Archiving

The set of data and information collected must be ordered and preserved to document the identification activity of things, thus building a museum archive, which is available to the team, but also the public, the scholars and those who will continue the work in the near or remote future.

After such a multifaceted deep process of knowing objects and the related creation of cataloguing cards, students have a full possession and awareness of school heritage with which they came into contact. This is certainly a large complex operation, which requires time and preliminary preparation by teachers, who guide this pedagogical cataloguing activity, but it can leave an incisive cultural (as well as experiential) trace in students.

The Turin School Museum Network

The guidelines developed by *La Scuola è il nostro Patrimonio* have inspired the project *Vuoi costruire il tuo museo scolastico?* (Do you want to develop your own school museum?), which was promoted by the Archives, Museums and Cultural Heritage Service of the Municipality of Turin, and the Strumento Testa Association, to enable any school interested in creating its own school museum to find a dedicated support over time[72]. This project has developed a step-by-step working method to support teachers in creating a school museum with their students, starting with a training course on the subject, then followed by *I sette passi per realizzare il museo scolastico* (Seven Steps to Create your Museum). Launched in 2011, the project has over the years attracted many participations and has thus encouraged and supported the creation of various museums in the Turin area[73]. The plurality of experiences and the awareness of the need for a continuous study of this heritage led the schools that had created a school museum to want to have a structured opportunity to meet, exchange, and study in depth (Periotto, Pizzigoni, & Treccarichi 2021), so they created the "School Museum Network" on November 2nd, 2015[74]. This had been firstly coordinated by "Gabelli School" and then by "Cena School" starting from 2021 and it is configured as a network open to all the schools working on their historical educational heritage with a view to its valorisation and educational use through an active

---

[72] See URL: <http://www.comune.torino.it/museiscuola/partecipa/vuoi-costruire-il-tuo-museo-scolastico.shtml> (24.11.2021).

[73] The list of school museums and their first information are available at: <http://www.comune.torino.it/museiscuola/propostemusei/rete-scolastica-dedicata-al-tema-dei-musei-scolast-2.shtml> (24.11.2021).

[74] The *Network Agreement among schools*, at the base of the Turin School Museum Network, is available on the webpage: <http://www.comune.torino.it/museiscuola/bm~doc/accordo_di-_rete.pdf> (24.11.2021).

involvement course of students and teachers in all the stages. This Network felt the need to equip itself with a shared tool for studying, inventorying, and cataloguing its historical-educational heritage with the support of the City of Turin (Ortolano & Treccarichi 2021) and INDIRE[75]. In fact, cataloguing meant bringing to light and giving dignity to a previously hidden and forgotten heritage; it meant understanding the global corpus of its school historical assets; it meant being able to communicate them externally too, offering a lot of ideas, from the possibility of creating new educational activities based on certain assets to the possibility of attracting the attention of some former students or scholars, creating collaborations with other bodies, and so on. It was decided to try to design a cataloguing tool for the network, which is able to be configured as a set of different realities: each of them has its own heritage, but with common objectives and working methods.

Therefore, the idea was a common repository, which would allow us to create a virtual place where the assets of each school would become a "common heritage" while remaining clearly traceable to the owning school. In this way, each school could create the cataloguing of its own assets and have its own inventory at any time but, at the same time, it could also study its own materials in the light of the heritage belonging to other local schools and the entire network's assets. At the same time, the Network and its members could also benefit from a uniform cataloguing system, which is able to make the cataloguing cards of different realities dialogue.

The challenges, which this proposal posed, were threefold:

---

[75] The text of the *Memorandum of Understanding* between the City of Turin and the Turin School Museum Network is available on the webpage: <http://www.comune.torino.it/museiscuola/bm~doc/1_prot_musei-scolas-tici_2016.pdf> (24.11.2021).

– identifying a cataloguing card for each asset, which could respond to the needs of knowing assets, but it was suitable for the educational work, which was directly carried out with students;

– establishing a categorization of assets, which is able to respond to scientific criteria and, at the same time, to be a real answer to the school needs;

– identifying the most suitable and accessible IT solution.

It may not be useless to share the process of creating this repository of school heritage, also highlighting the difficulties they had, the mistakes they made and the needs, which are strongly expressed by schools with respect to this tool, in order to offer those who would carry out similar projects a ground for discussion from which to start in the future. In the experience of the Turin School Museum Network, small steps were taken with the aim of developing a non-definitive experimental tool, which was ready to compare with various project partners at any time, working according to a principle of field verification and progressive development. Clear aspects were the needs from which they started and, at the same time, the theoretical and technical difficulties to be solved that are attributable to the lack of a legal recognition or, in any case, of a globally accepted definition of the "school heritage" category (Brunelli 2013). In the first case, it was a question of identifying criteria, which were rigorous, unambiguous, non-subjective and, at the same time, suitable to the needs of different schools. On the other hand, a technical question arose: do they have to design a specific software or test one, which was already in use, but modifiable according to specific needs and the ones which could emerge during the experimentation? This last question was answered by making use of INDIRE technologists and, specifically, by referring to the experience and equipment linked to the "Immersive Teaching" project, which was coordinated by the researcher Andrea Benassi. His field research, thanks to which he had supported various schools in educational activities related to the technological field, had led to the identification and use of a modifiable open-source software to lean on. Instead, with respect to the structure of various categories of school heritage, the categorization hypothesis promoted by Juri Meda (2010) was very useful for reflection and proposed a subdivision among architectural assets, artistic assets (works of art, which were produced and/or preserved in schools), teaching assets – that is, teaching aids for teaching various disciplines, which can be therefore divided into musical assets; scientific, technological and naturalistic assets; mathematical and/or geometric assets; geographical assets, gymnastic assets –, pedagogical assets (for example, Froebelian, Montessorian materials..) and, finally, material assets, which have been stratified within the institutes over time, such as furniture, stationery, clothes, radios, projectors etc., in addition to archival and book assets.

By comparing schools and accepting their request to base on the set of assets, which Meda names "teaching assets", as a priority, we tried to create a list of possible teaching assets relating to each discipline – being inspired by the categorization, offered by the historical catalogues of companies producing teaching aids –. The hypothesis was that the compiler would start the action of entering the information of each object starting from the discipline so that the system would respond after selecting it by showing the list of possible assets relating to that discipline in a drop-down menu. In this way, the compiler was thought to be facilitated in the action of identifying and entering the data into the card. However, during the first test, we realised that the list of possible assets was excessively long, particularly in terms of technical-graphic efficiency (a *non user friendly* drop-down menu), with the result of creating confusion. It was decided to transform the phase of setting up the cataloguing structure into action-research when INDIRE researchers entered the classroom. This allowed them to directly and indirectly observe the *modus operandi* of schools working on historical educational assets. This included both the work of classes within the school museum, struggling with the "knowledge" of each object, and the indirect work through the study of the school assets' description cards, produced by schools.

The collection of these data allowed a subsequent work of synthesis between the spontaneous method, which is used by schools (therefore, it responded to the school need), and the need for univocal criteria, which would allow an empirical classification of school heritage. The macro-data, which emerged from observation, showed how their typology and use guided the action of schools to identify/catalogue assets and made historical pedagogical objects immediately recognisable/usable for pupils and teachers. Objects were questioned by schools following the questions "what is it?", "what kind of object is it?" and, then, the name of the object, the discipline to which it pertains, etc. came from these questions. Therefore, first of all, schools felt the need to start from a different (non-disciplinary) categorization, which was closer to the heuristic approach they used. Then, we proceeded to test a structure, which would allow entering data from a different categorization, which is able to privilege the kind of object, as it emerged from the observation of the classes working. Furthermore, starting from a criterion, which was not strictly disciplinary, it was possible to expand the action of cataloguing assets, also including school furniture and aids, which were intended as objects of daily use within school life, such as inkwells, nibs, etc.

Therefore, the macro-categories chosen were:

1. School furniture;

2. Students' works;

3. Aids;

4. Teaching tools.

For the latter, a further test phase highlighted how the breadth of different assets, which could be counted as teaching tools, created difficulties for schools both by not supporting them in the identification of some assets as part of the heritage and by not facilitating them in the identification of a name, which could be shared by all the members of the Network. For this reason, we tried to extrapolate a set of sub-categories from an analysis of the collections inside the schools participating in the experimentation. In this way, after selecting the "teaching tools" category, the system proposed to indicate the subcategory by selecting it among:

5. Educational wall boards (both in relief and bidimensional);

6. Pedagogical boxes with samples of materials;

7. Taxidermied animals;

8. School typography (including both the typographical types with the related boxes and the machines for reprographics);

9. Montessorian materials;

10. Froebelian materials;

11. Models (of anatomical, botanical nature)

12. Boxes with educational games;

13. Geometric solids;

14. Technical/scientific instruments [*strumentaria*][76]: including all *chemistry* and *physics* instruments (from microscopes to solvents, Newton discs, hearing aids, just to give some examples), but also *drawing* instruments (for example, the pyrography) or instruments relating to the *technological* area (old recorders or computers).

This general scheme allowed us to have a structure that was suitable for all the schools and their collections. This structure was able to be a supporting element for connecting all the cards of each object, which were produced by schools and then associated with categories. Starting from this affiliation of each object to its category and subcategory, a specific cataloguing card of the object was then created. The identification/cataloguing card of each asset was structured as follows:

1. name of the object;

2. discipline;

3. year of creation;

4. manufacturing company;

5. materials with which it is made;

---

[76] The term "strumentaria" ["instruments"] was borrowed from the nomenclature proposed by the working group in *Cose di Scienze* (Science's Stuff), a project coordinated by the Polytechnic of Turin, which had just carried out a census of historical-scientific educational assets in the previous year. See (Marchis, 2014).

6. school to which it belongs (with the related field specifying the Educational Directorate to which this school belongs and the city);

7. image of the object (several images can be uploaded);

8. description field of the object;

9. notes (e.g., inventory label on the object).

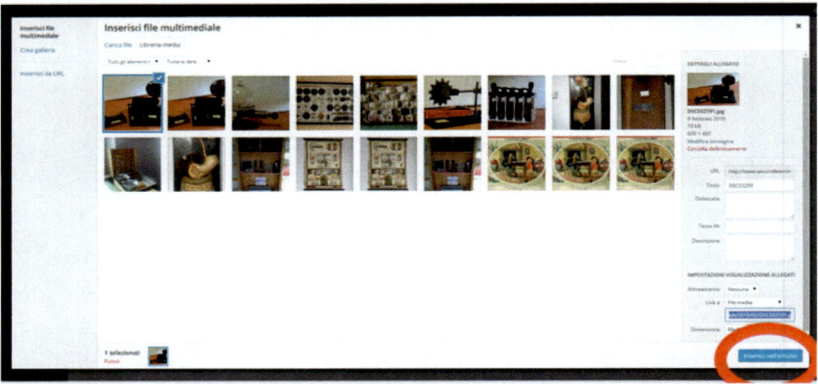

Pic. 5.5. *Image of the back end for the pedagogical cataloguing system of the historical educational heritage, which was developed for the project*

The system allowed carrying out research in the front-end using search keys:

10. categories (for example, all the school furniture);

11. subcategories (for example, all the educational display boards);

12. discipline (all the objects relating to Geography);

13. each school (all the objects belonging to Sclopis school, for example);

14. year of creation;

15. manufacturing company.

The experimentation was carried out in 2015 and 2016 and saw the participation of all the schools belonging to the Turin School Museum Network and the results of the activity were the subject of a presentation as part of the Congress SEPHE-*Sociedad Española para el Estudio del Patrimonio Histórico-Educativo,* held in San Sebastian in 2016 (Pizzigoni 2016). There were some critical issues, which were attributable to the need for verification and control of data, which were entered by external experts in order to review the cards; different languages and styles when describing assets; long times required for teaching work, which must be naturally reconciled with the overall needs of the class. The most serious difficulty was linked to the obsolescence of the chosen IT system, which was no longer updated and, therefore, no longer usable[77].

This experience led to a broader and more detailed reflection.

First of all, it allowed us to reflect on the breadth of this kind of pedagogical cataloguing action with respect to the growth of the students' knowledge and competences: the activity is intrinsically interdisciplinary; it facilitates lessons, which are based on the use of new technologies; it represents an exercise in writing (and, therefore, in the Italian language), as well as identifying information and summarizing it; it leads to historical knowledge with respect to history of the disciplines and their tools, but also indirectly economic, industrial and commercial history linked to the manu-

---

[77] The heritage of this experience is collected by a current educational cataloguing activity the Turin School Museum Network is carrying out through a cataloguing grid, which is developed with the collaboration of the archivists from the Culture Department of the City of Turin.

facturing realities of these objects, which students are cataloguing, and history of their own school, which has collected these materials over the years. With respect to competences, just think about observation, finding information, contextualization and procedural skills, which this kind of activity requires from students.

A second area of reflection concerns the topic of in-service teachers' training and, specifically, how a pedagogical cataloguing project also requires teachers to make an effort to study and train new topics, in particular through an online repository, thus also offering an opportunity for personal and professional development.

Finally, a more systemic reflection better embraces the needs of studying school historical heritage: we questioned whether it was scientifically correct that students "catalogued" these assets or it would have been more appropriate to rely on an external expert, who could catalogue all the assets of the schools belonging to the Network on a common *repository* in a more complete, uniform and scientific manner for the purpose of implementing the repository. These are naturally two totally different kinds of activities and have a vision and an approach relating to different objectives at their base. The scientific efficiency and, at the same time, the optimization of time compared to the choice of an external expert would be also undoubted. But, beyond the value of the educational benefits, which we have seen with an activity like this one experimented by the Turin School Museum Network, , a broader analysis shows that a census/cataloguing of school historical heritage cannot be limited to a few schools. In our opinion, it is only possible by actively involving multiple actors and 'cataloguers', represented by each school with its teachers and students. This operation exposes the possibility of mistakes, long times and various kinds of difficulties on the one hand and it can be very incisive on the other hand precisely because it requires a very deep preliminary preparation and appropriation phase of its own school assets, which represents the only way for a real widespread operation of "education to school heritage" and also the only one which creates a long-term widespread consciousness of this heritage as well as awareness by schools, which are its guardians.

The "Patrimoniere"

Since 2019 the fundings offered by ministerial PONs (National Operational Programmes), and especially the one dedicated to the "Enhancement of education on cultural, artistic and landscape heritage", has allowed the Turin School Museum Network to experiment with a new working method involving the same heritage expert. A direct link has been established with the students in the classroom (and not only with the teachers, as in the project *Vuoi costruire il tuo museo scolastico?*) and a specific educational path of 30 hours has been organised based on the students' direct approach to school heritage. One of these modules led to the birth of the figure of the *Patrimonieri*, that is students who are invested with the title of "heritage experts", who know the "secrets" of their school's heritage and go so far as to create a school museum with classmates through a path, which starts from the first recognition and discovery of their own school heritage (Pizzigoni 2021 and 2022a). Among the various stages of the *Patrimonieri*'s journey to acquire the knowledge that will enable them to create a museum, there is a stage dedicated to pedagogical cataloguing, that is, working in direct contact with the school material that the students have to identify and catalogue.

The working method that characterises all the *Patrimoniere*'s path requires students to be directly put "in the situation", that is, in direct contact with the object they have to catalogue and in a research community that co-constructs knowledge[78]. The work is carried out cooperatively and includes a final review and development phase with the whole class group. The cataloguing activity is done on different kinds of material related to the category of school heritage, for each of which there is a specific card, called "the radar of the Patrimoniere". The aim is to guide the pupils in their observation, to make them feel supported and to allow them to move in the process of approaching an unknown heritage.

In addition to the card, students are supported by two other aids in this identification phase: sharing copies of historical catalogues from companies producing teaching aids and using internet and technologies to identify films or cards, which help understand the use of teaching objects, the discipline to which they refer, any physical or chemical laws showing other elements, which can help in dating.

Since the elements to be observed in different categories of assets (objects, books, exercise books, documents) are different, a basic card (which can be adapted and improved each time) was created for each of them. Below are the specific cards for each category of material heritage with which these "Patrimonieri" work to offer an outline, which is adaptable according to the needs of each school.

---

[78] We refer to the *Knowledge building community* and the 12 principles underlying it according to the promoters Scardamalia and Bereiter: real ideas-authentic problems; improvement of ideas; diversity of ideas; higher summary points; epistemic activation; knowledge of the community as a collective responsibility; democratization of knowledge; symmetrical advances in knowledge; knowledge construction as a pervasive process; constructive use of authoritative sources; speech focused on knowledge construction; distributed transformative assessment. See Scardamalia & Bereiter (2006).

Pic. 5.6 *"Patrimonieri" at Gabelli primary school in Turin working on their school historical photographs*

Pic. 5.7 *and* **5.8** *"Patrimonieri" at the "Cena" primary school in Turin showing visitors the result of their work on historical school exercise book, which were found at school*

How to catalogue an exercise book

- school year;

- school;

- class;

- the student's name;

- discipline;

- cover: *writing down if there is an image and what it represents; if there is the name of whoever produced the exercise book (do you know that exercise books were sometimes used for advertising or making Geography or History known? Oh, yes! They were really "talking" objects);*

- particular contents: *Did a topic or a content inside it strike you? Which homework did the students who owned this exercise book do?;*

- particular marks: *writings, stains, grades;*

- drawings made by students.

How to catalogue a photograph

- year when it was taken;

- the class represented (if it is a class photo);

- the school represented (if it is a photo depicting a school context);

- place;

- particular marks on the photo (is there anything written on the back? Is there the name of the photographer or the student who owns it?...);

- particular contents of the photo: *are there any details within the image, which reveal something interesting to us, in your opinion? For example, do they point out what school was like in the past? Or, what kind of activities did pupils do? Or, how many pupils were in the class? Let's write everything down: "Patrimonieri", don't skip any clues!*

How to catalogue a book

- title;

- discipline;

- year;

- publishing house;

- place;

- particular marks: *there are writings, notes, the owner's name, etc.;*

- *images: are there photographs or drawings? Which style do they have? Is there the illustrator's name?;*

- *Patrimoniere's notes: did anything about this book strike you? The cover, for example? Or, does it have any strange content, which surprised you?*

How to catalogue a school object

- name of the object (or name hypothesis, if we don't know it);

- reference discipline (is it for Science? Geography? Other?);

- year of production/production period (also hypothesised or reconstructed through someone's memories. If it is a hypothesis, we write it in brackets: you know well that the "Patrimonieri" are precise and do not want to confuse reliable data with the hypothesised ones);

- manufacturing company (if you're lucky, there is a label on the object with the name of the person who made it);

- particular marks (are there any traces, writings or anything else? Inventory number, labels?);

- what was it for? (An experiment at school? A particular lesson?);

- memories linked to that object: (perhaps, former teachers or pupils remember some episodes linked to that object).

How to catalogue a document

- Type of document;

- Who created/produced it;

- Who is it addressed to?;

- Production place;

- Year;

- Subject of the document (write which is the topic in a few words);

- Description of the contents after "studying" the document;

- Particular marks (drawings, notes, stains …);

- "Secrets about school", which the document reveals.

Pic. 5.9 *and* **5.10** *"Patrimonieri" at the "Lessona" primary school in Turin working on historical pedagogical objects, which were found in their school*

It is evident that we are far from real cataloguing, and it is rather a tool, which is designed to facilitate the process of approaching and knowing assets or "identifying" them, if we want to use a term, which has been previously introduced. On the other hand, it is true that without this simple action, there is no way to move to the deeper levels of understanding assets, nor to initiate the process of interpretation. This process represents "a form of education, similar to heritage education, as it aims not only to transmit knowledge, but has the ultimate goal of training a visitor [in this case, a learner] who appreciates the value of the heritage, and, above all, a competent user of it" (Brunelli 2018, pp. 44-45).

The NEMO project of the network of Historical Schools in Naples

The Association of the Historical Schools in Naples was born in September 2011 as a network project, which gathers the centenarian schools of all levels in Naples. Under Francesco Di Vaio's coordination, schools gathered in a common path for enhancing their cultural heritage through the reorganization and the cataloguing of school archives and libraries and, finally, the creation of museum areas in schools[79]. Since its creation, the network has promoted various initiatives, such as training events, preparation of exhibitions, organization of conferences and printing of catalogues and publications for disseminating the results of the research and teaching work, which has been undertaken by school community in collaboration with the area (Di Vaio 2014 and 2017)[27].

---

[79] Further information and documents are available on the Neapolitan Historical Schools Forum website: <http://www.forumscuolestorichenapole-tane.it/> (01.09.2022).

Pic. 5.11. *Homepage of the Project NEMO-Network Educational Museums online for cataloguing the historical museum heritage of scientific tools in the Historical Schools of Naples.*[80]

The subsequent project stands out among the actions developed and was launched by six schools[81], which drew up the Network Agreement NEMO-*Network Educational Museums Online* in collaboration with *Associazione Scienza e scuola* (founded by Professor Paolo Strolin)[82] and the support of the Municipality of Naples and the Department of Physics at Federico II University of Naples in the years 2013-2016. NEMO was created with the specific aim of safeguarding and making available the rich historical-scientific heritage preserved by Neapolitan schools, consisting of physics

---

80

[81] The first school network is made up of: "Vittorio Emanuele II" Classical High School, "Della Porta-Porzio" State Technical Institute, "Gian Battista Vico" State High School, "Elena di Savoia" State Institute of Higher Education, "Pasquale Villari" State High School and "Alessandro Volta" State Industrial Technical Institute. See *La rete Nemo*, in <http://progettonemo.it/index.php?pg=8> (12.12.2021).

[82] See the association's website: <https://www.scienzaescuola.eu/> (01.09.2022).

instruments, naturalistic finds, animals, minerals and rocks dating back to the House of Bourbon and post-unification periods. For this purpose, the project implements all the necessary recovery, restoration, conservation and cataloguing activities for the heritage with the relative publication of cards, which are produced within a specifically designed and created multimedia catalogue online (<http://progettonemo.it/>). The project is coordinated by Mrs. Gioia Molisso, a Physics teacher at "Vittorio Emanuele II-Garibaldi" Classical High School, who oversaw the inventorying and cataloguing operations for the prestigious scientific cabinet of her institute together with her students.

NEMO led to the creation of two fundamental results: the first one is represented by the *digital Museum online*, which allows sharing online photos and cards of over 800 catalogued tools - also accessible through a paper catalogue since 2019 - and is supported by a special platform, which was designed for this purpose (Molisso 2019). The second result of the project is represented by changing the historical aids, which are preserved in the Neapolitan schools, from antiquarian objects, as they had been considered for years, to tools for the implementation of a new science teaching in which students played a leading role: in fact, the great added value of the project is that all the activities are directly managed by school community, and have an important educational and training impact on students.

The 2015 Scientific Tools Exhibition

In 2015, NEMO project group created at the National Library in the Royal Palace of Naples the exhibition *Strumenti Scientifici dai Borbone all'Epoca Post-Unitaria. La Fisica nelle Scuole Napoletane dell'Ottocento* (Scientific Instruments from the Bourbon Era to the Post-Unification Period. The Study of Physics in Neapolitan Schools of the 19th Century).

For the creation of the exhibition, students collaborated in cleaning, restarting and preparing the tools to be put on display with the aim of showing not only the beauty, but also the modernity of these «exceptional teaching tools, which were frequently used in school laboratories for understanding classical science» (Molisso & Cavaliere 2019, p. 44). Finally, students were called to play the role of scientific divulgers and, in this capacity, they introduced not only the historical tools to the public, but they also carried out some experiments aimed at demonstrating how these tools worked. In particular, these experiments were filmed with the collaboration of the National Institute for Nuclear Physics of Naples: the produced videos were projected during the exhibition and, therefore, made public through the YouTube channel.

Pathways for transversal skills and orientation (the former School-Work Alternation project)

After the experience gained during the 2015 exhibition, the working group presented a proposal for the ministerial project PCTO-*Percorsi per le Competenze Trasversali e per l'Orientamento* (Pathways for Transversal Skills and Orientation, formerly known as the School-Work Alternation project). The proposal focused specifically on the historical tools of the schools participating in the NEMO network, and included the following theoretical and practical activities:

1) Firstly, students dealt with the correct "historical framework of the collections of scientific tools, the study of the

physical principles relating to the tools, etc." (Molisso & Cavaliere 2019, p. 45);

2) Therefore, they acquired a specific training on the basic principles of restoration and conservation, the fundamentals for cataloguing naturalistic finds and scientific tools, the functioning of the NEMO database;

3) Finally, they devoted themselves to carry out various activities ranging from the restoration operations to the drafting of cards for tools, the creation and processing of digital photographs and the creation of videos with experiments, which were carried out with the same historical scientific tools in order to illustrate how they worked (Molisso 2021b).

Therefore, the produced audiovisual materials were disseminated on the YouTube channel linked to the NEMO project platform. The channel is continuously enriched, collecting up to 115 educational videos including 27 videos, which were made by students during Alternating School-Work activities, and 37 videos about physics experiments, which were made in collaboration with the National Institute for Nuclear Physics of Naples, as mentioned[83].

As Prof. Molisso underlines, these activities are particularly «suitable for daily life» (Molisso 2021b, p. 645) of young people precisely for their multimediality, facilitating the acquisition of interdisciplinary and transversal knowledge and skills. Over the years, the project has been further developing leading to the implementation

---

[83] See *Alternanza Scuola-Lavoro con Nemo*, on the YouTube Channel: *Progetto Nemo- Network Educational Museums Online*, <https://www.youtube.com/channel/UCODqbNUA66EkwW1okwmnVKQ> (15.01.2022).

of the *Museopedia* website, which is completely devoted to Vittorio Emanuele-Garibaldi Liceo and its collections where it is possible to take a virtual tour of the Physics and Natural Sciences school museums (Pic. 5.12). Three different classes (*ibid.*, p. 648), who planned the virtual visit and created all the multimedia materials (from the images to the videos of scientific experiments and the audio descriptions of the texts), worked on the platform – whose creation was started with PCTO in 2017, continued with PON *Musei scientifici del Vittorio Emanuele II* in 2019 and the same path in 2020, 2021 and 2022.

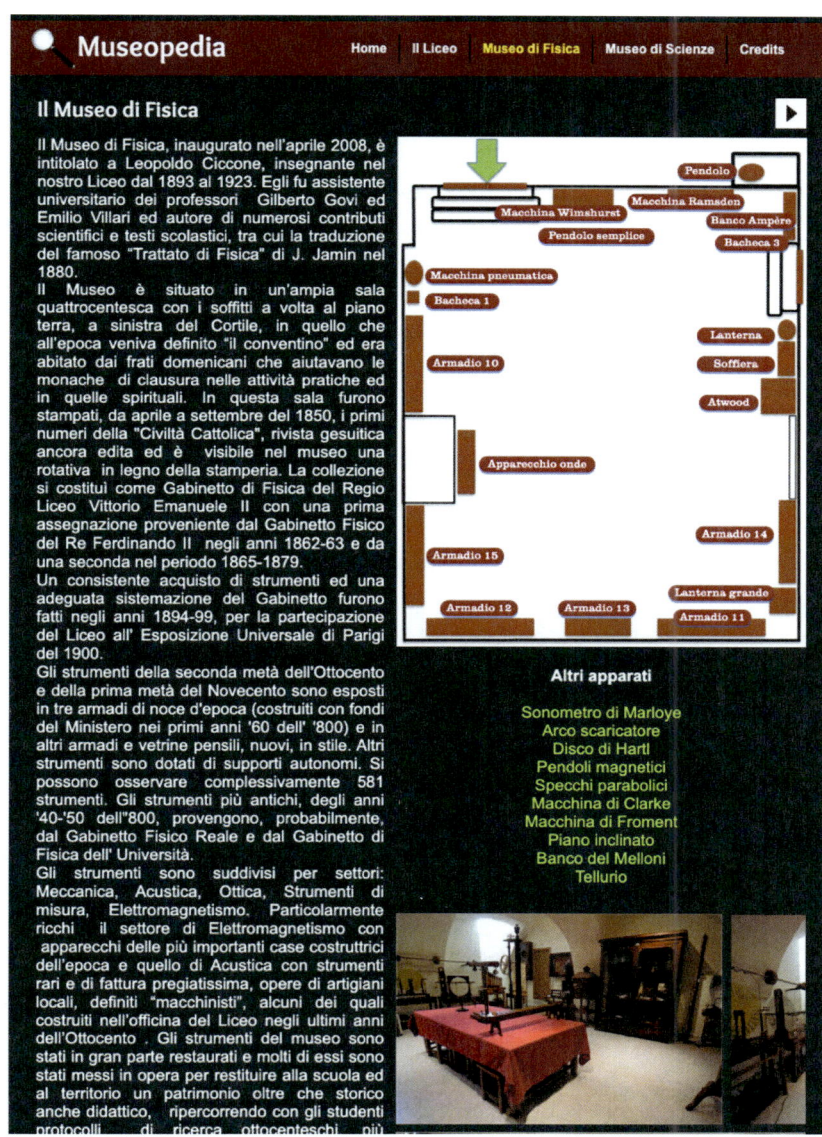

Pic. 5.12. *The Physics Museum on Museopedia: <https://www.museopedia.net/>* (18.10.2022)

Thanks to the positive results obtained, the teaching model, which has been tested in the above-illustrated paths, has been definitively consolidated in the new 2022/2025 Three-Year Study Plan at Vittorio Emanuele II-Garibaldi Classical High School of Naples, as confirmed by the PCTOs linked to the Project of cataloguing the school scientific heritage: *Students@Nemo: un percorso di lavoro attraverso Scienza, Storia e Tecnologia*. Thus, the objectives for protecting, cataloguing and preserving the scientific heritage belonging to NEMO School Network are linked to the training mission of a modern school, which is in step with the times and able to safeguard the heritage and, at the same time, to transmit disciplinary, transversal, technological and professionalizing knowledge and skills linked to contemporaneity.

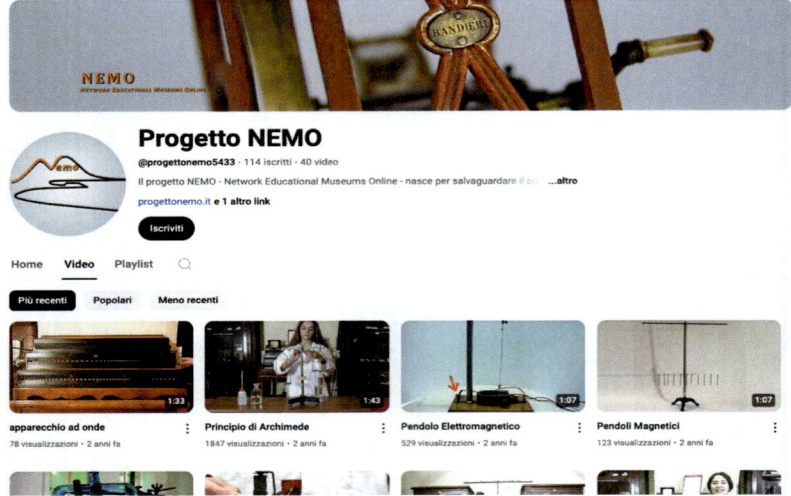

Pic. 5.13. *NEMO Project YouTube channel, <https://www.youtube.com/channel/UCODqbNUA66EkwW1okwmnVKQ> (18.10.2022)*

The Museum Online

The census and cataloguing of historical-scientific heritage, which is preserved in the historical schools of Naples, was the guiding idea, which oriented the birth and development of all the project. Therefore, the Museum online was the end point of the above-illustrated activities and the realization of the pre-established objectives of protecting, cataloguing and spreading information on the heritage studied. The web application, which was appropriately designed, allowed computerised cataloguing through the collection of the following information:

- name,

- historical period,

- production materials,

- dimensions,

- manufacturer,

- state of conservation,

- description and use,

- notes,

- sources,

- references to previous inventories,

- photographs and illustrations.

The application allows the inclusion of cards into the database and the public use of data. In the latter case, the user interface has a different introduction of the information to be displayed in relation to different purposes of the project: 1) making information relating to the owned scientific tools accessible to everyone; 2) promoting the museum network; 3) doing scientific divulgation on the web with the support of the Facebook page and the YouTube channel.

For this purpose, the user interface allows us to consult the catalogue online through three different tools, which are: *Inventory*, *Gallery* and *Research* (Pics. 5.14-16). These tools allow us to visualize a specific tool among the ones listed in the Inventory, to explore the school materials in the catalogue within a specific disciplinary field of interest (for example, in the Optics or Natural Sciences *category*, etc.), or to carry out research through the appropriate query mask by selecting a single field or combining the four fields available: *category, historical period, manufacturer, keywords*. Among them, the first two fields have pre-filled values (which can be selected from the drop-down menu), while the last two fields are free-hand entries.

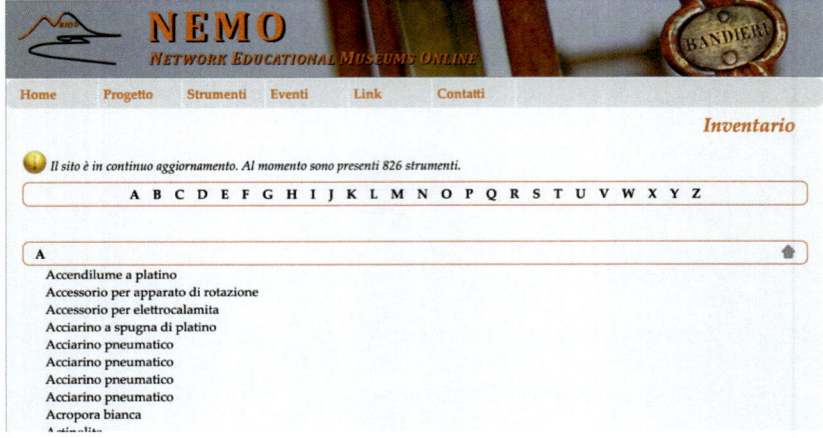

Pic. 5.14. *Tools of the query mask of the online catalogue of the museum*

Pic. 5.15. *Gallery of categories*

Pic. 5.16. *Search fields*

The query mask was organised in an extremely functional way in its simplicity and clarity and allows us to carry out different kinds of research.

The display mask (Pic. 5.17) is also clear because the image of each tool is accompanied by the necessary information, which is furnished with a bibliography and/or external links.

This database is an example of how it is possible to implement an essential IT infrastructure, which allows a simple management and use for schools where most of these materials are preserved today, while containing all the necessary data for the correct description of assets at the same time. A cataloguing system that is simple to maintain and easy to use for teachers and students will greatly facilitate data entry and database management. Above all, it will serve the two main purposes of pedagogical cataloguing:

1) offering students a complete training course, which combines the theoretical study of school disciplines with the experimental component (study and use of historical scientific aids), research (study and collection of sources), the acquisition of the necessary digital skills for the creation of a digital artefact (digitised cataloguing and audiovisual aids);

2) safeguarding the school heritage by enhancing it through the public communication of science and, finally, promoting knowledge and respect for that heritage, for the history of the school and the area where it is located among young people and citizens.

Lanterna da proiezione

Categoria: Ottica
Periodo Storico: Fine XIX - Inizio XX Secolo
Costruttore: Ed. Liesegang, Dusseldorf
Materiali: Lamiera in ferro, ottone, vetro, porcellana
Dimensioni: 56cm x 50cm x 22cm
Stato di Conservazione: Buono
Funzionante: Si
Descrizione: La lanterna da proiezione è una diretta discendente della lanterna magica, strumento per proiettare su una superficie immagini dipinte o fotografiche, fisse o a movimento manuale, in modo da consentire la visione a più persone contemporaneamente. Le parti fondamentali della lanterna sono costituite da una fonte luminosa, un condensatore di luce e un obiettivo, più o meno complesso. La lanterna è pervenuta completa di ottiche. Probabilmente si tratta di una lanterna ad arco modificata, come si evince dalla presenza della canna fumaria. La lanterna è corredata da passavedute. I passavedute venivano utilizzati per posizionare i vetri da proiezione della lanterna in occasione di uno spettacolo, di una conferenza o di una lezione. Esisteva anche la versione singola, ma il passavedute doppio fu generalmente preferito perché consentiva la sostituzione dell'immagine senza interrompere la sequenza della proiezione. La lanterna presenta lateralmente un interruttore in porcellana bianca; il filo di alimentazione è originale come la lampada di illuminazione.
Note: Raphael Eduard Liesegang (Elberfeld, 1° novembre 1869 – Bad Homburg vor der Höhe, 13 novembre 1947) è stato un chimico fotografo e imprenditore tedesco..
Fonti: L.Mannoni, "La grande arte della luce e dell'ombra", Lindau, Torino, 2000.
www.uibk.ac.at.it
Mannoni, L. (a cura di), "Le mouvement continué: catalogue illustré de la collection des appareils de la Cinemathéque francaise", Milano, Mazzotta,

Pic. 5.1 *Visualizing a catalogue card from Museum Online*

The Historical School heritage: Between teaching science and teaching Old Greek

The spirit that drove the NEMO project and the educational activities, which that have developed since the creation of the Neapolitan schools' network was already captured in an interesting interdisciplinary educational path that Prof. Molisso had created with her students at the Vittorio Emanuele II Classical High School in previous years. Together with her colleague Livia Marrone, a teacher of Classical Languages at the same school, she collaborated with the Study Department for the Ancient Classical and Mediterranean World at the University of Naples "L'Orientale" to create an educational path. This path successfully achieved the goal of establishing a dialogue between two seemingly unrelated disciplines, Greek and Physics, by starting precisely from the ancient scientific tools preserved in school museums.

Under the guidance of the two teachers, the students have explored the passages from the *Pneumatica* of Heron of Alexandria (1ˢᵗ century AD), where the Greek mathematician and mechanic described the hydraulic device he designed, which took the name of Heron's Fountain. By directly comparing various passages of the ancient source with the material structure of the teaching aid preserved in the school museum, students were able to grasp the theoretical principles, which were taken from the text through their application with the aim of putting the ancient machinery back into action (Marrone & Molisso 2011).

The same teaching model was applied in a subsequent project, which was developed from an article written in 1936 and found in the 1936-1937 issue of the School Yearbook. In his article *Un'ora di studio e di pazienza seguendo un'esperienza di fisica* (An hour of study and patience during a physics experience), the student Giorgio Tufari described a physics experiment carried out by a group of third-class students and their teacher, using the old *Hope Apparatus* still kept in the school's Physics Cabinet. The students, guided by their teacher, successfully reproduced the experiment. After making some necessary adaptations, due to the ancient apparatus's conditions and the evolution of modern measuring tools, an educational experience took place. Moreover, the experience was enriched by the emotional burden experienced by students who identified with the school life of their peers from long ago (Molisso 2021a).

From this brilliant example, it is possible to understand how many and which disciplinary intersections the pedagogical cataloguing of school heritage can lead to, if applied with intelligence, sensitivity and creativity.

Conclusions

As seen from the above-illustrated experiences, the pedagogical cataloguing of school historical heritage can become the fulcrum of a network of activities and mobilize various interdisciplinary skills and knowledge characterizing all the school curriculum in both a transversal and vertical sense since it involves an activity, which can be developed by students coming from schools of all levels – with different kinds of deep examination –. Some strengths as well as some critical issues, which we will try to summarize, have emerged from the experiences described.

The first strength is represented by the positive impact on learning and teaching, which projects of cataloguing and research on school heritage can have in terms of educational impact and commitment of the children involved in the activities. Whether using a playful approach (which is more appropriate for the first school levels) or a more scientific and exhaustive approach at a level of technical-specialist knowledge (which is more suited to higher education), working on the objects of school historical heritage allows going beyond, focusing the transmission of knowledge and skills on a single field of knowledge to then extend to many other disciplinary fields: from the historical-humanistic field up to the technological IT field.

The impacts, which such projects have on the community are also important.

As we have seen, various educational and cultural activities can arise around the knowledge of school assets (and the school, which produced, used and preserved them). On the one hand, they assign a finally active role to teachers, students, families, even entire neighbourhoods as happened in the project at XXV Aprile School in Turin (Pizzigoni 2013) up to all the municipal area in the recovery and valorisation operations of a heritage for which they feel responsible. On the other hand, they end up generating a sense of protection towards that heritage in all the actors involved together with a greater cohesion of a wider community, who revolves around the school micro-community.

A final strength is represented by the cultural and scientific impacts, which saving school heritage (which is potentially always in danger) can generate in terms of sharing data and information: the publication of databases through websites or specific computerised cataloguing platforms allows all the national and international scientific community to especially access new sources and give a new impetus to specialist research.

Despite many strengths, there are some important critical issues to be dealt with for those who wish to undertake a pedagogical cataloguing project of their school heritage. First, a unique system is necessary for data, which are collected at a minimal level and must comply with some minimum quality, homogeneity and interoperability requirements, allowing comparison and fusion with other databases, where possible. Finally, the online publication of the cataloguing results is a fundamental prerequisite since the results of the work are visible to the school community, the headquarters of the project, other school communities and, finally, the scientific community. For this purpose, a unique cataloguing system should be made available to all the schools, based on a free software, devoted to schools and, therefore, easy to use for teachers and students, possibly online so that the results (the catalogued assets) are visible to the community, and finally managed by an authority, who can ensure constant scientific support both at a technological and technical-scientific level and at a level of continuously training teachers on the management of school heritage and cataloguing skills.

We are aware of the long times and the difficulties, which such a path has on multiple fronts. In the awareness that many obstacles will have to be faced and overcome – *in primis* the development of univocal criteria for cataloguing school objects –, before arriving at these results, we humbly take the liberty of indicating some initial preparatory objectives, which we believe they can be achieved in the medium term, such as:

- a census of school projects and/or websites, which worked on cataloguing their heritage;

- the creation of a platform for sharing already available resources (e.g., catalogues, cards, historical sources, etc.).

The hope is that new and even more productive synergies will come to life in the coming years – thanks also to the support, which SIPSE Society has already given and will continue to give, and the consequent scientific *know-how*, which the university world will increasingly be able to offer in this perspective –, in order to give a concrete form to that idea of *school museum*, which Hugues de Varine had proposed in 1978 as a reality, which was able to create a deep «interaction between school structure and community» through «the use of all the museographic activities for educational purposes and the young people's sensitization for all the problems raised and the processes of community development» (De Varine 2005b, p. 269)[41].

De Varine goes to more specifically analyse the reality of a *school museum* – «whether or not it is open to the extra-school community» (De Varine 2005c, p. 168)[42] – as one of many possible declinations of an *ecomuseum*. Of course, the *school museum*, which the French museologist describes, is not the museum of school historical heritage yet, but it prefigures and summarizes all its potentials and features as a laboratory for students, a teaching tool at the service of teachers and a meeting place between school and community:

> The school museum is the result of a really museological process (initial conception, programming, setting up of rooms, identification and collection of objects, analysis and study, inventory, conservation, introduction, animation) linked to school activities in a cooperative way, associating parents, students and teachers (De Varine 2005c, p. 168). [...] [Its] advantages are various: offering teachers new educational tools, making parents aware of the importance of heritage (the family heritage or the environment heritage, for example) in their children's education inside and outside school and, finally, accustoming children to see in three dimensions, to touch and respect cultural heritage, to use it as an educational resource and a support for imagination and creativity since an early age, because the same object (*the real thing*, as referred by Duncan Cameron) can have various uses more or less linked to the school curriculum. The collection and juxtaposition of objects offer countless possibilities for expressing deduction and demonstration and is also a precious antidote to the hegemony of the image during the television era (*ibid.*, p. 169).

The passage evidently expresses the point of view of a man during the 1970s, as confirmed by that reference for the invitation «to see in three dimensions, to touch» as a real antidote against the «hegemony of the image during the television era». Although the warning inherent in that reflection was distant in time, it would maintain its importance and topical interest unchanged if only we replaced the words *image/television* with the words *virtual/network*: in fact, nowadays, during the web and social media era, educational work on real objects precisely seems to acquire a particular meaning not only as an «antidote» against the current *hegemony of the virtual over the real*, but rather as an educational activity, which is able to rebalance, enrich and complete contemporary education. In fact, the growing orientation of digital school towards technology and digital skills cannot overlook the risks of a new kind of 'manual illiteracy'. This includes the loss of fine motor skills and hand–eye coordination in younger generations, together with a significant decline in attention and concentration, which teachers and educators report every day. Therefore, the school museum puts itself up as an effective laboratory for the application and constant exercise of visual-manipulative skills and systematic observation activities and analysis of reality.

Finally, we add the fact that the museum – which is created at school, by school and for school – is also the expression of an extended community, as De Varine explains:

> The superiority of [creating] a school museum over traditional museum visits, where students are lined up in pairs, becomes immediately evident. This experience can also prepare students psychologically and intellectually for visiting a traditional museum, which they will eagerly anticipate and appreciate. This is because they will feel a

bit like the enlightened amateur who better understands
the professional's practice, having experienced firsthand
the difficulties and joys of this activity. Subsequently, this
same experience will foster the commitment of parents or
young adults, inspiring them to take charge of cultural
heritage in itself, and as a resource for their growth. Therefore, the school museum is a unique community museum,
as it is an emanation of the educational community as a
whole (De Varine 2005c, p. 169).

Collecting school historical heritage is an activity that can bring
the school community even closer to families, the area as well as
the world of culture, represented by heritage experts, historians,
conservators, museologists, and more. On the one hand, collecting,
analysing, and cataloguing significant materials (like the historical
school objects) lays the foundations for a school museum to serve
as a laboratory for cultivating various cultural and citizenship
skills. On the other hand, it creates a meeting place of identity for
diverse communities to connect and recognise each other through
school history and heritage.

Bibliography

Accogli, L., Nuzzo, P., & Marchiori, S. (2013). Il contributo dell'Orto Botanico dell'Università del Salento per la realizzazione di un museo storico-naturalistico nella scuola. *Museologia Scientifica. Nuova Serie, 7* (1/2), 143-150.

Alovisio, S. (2018). *La scuola dove si vede. Cinema ed educazione nell'Italia del primo Novecento.* Torino: Edizioni Kaplan.

Andreassi, R. (2013). I centri di ricerca e i Musei della scuola indicatori di sviluppo del rinnovamento storiografico. In H. Cavallera, ed., *La ricerca storico-educativa oggi. Un confronto di metodi, modelli e programmi di ricerca, 2 vols* (p. 175-192). Lecce: Pensa Multimedia.

Andreassi, R., & Barausse, A. (2020). Il «Museo della scuola e dell'educazione popolare» nel Sistema Museale dell'Università del Molise: tra pratiche storiografiche. Terza missione e sperimentazione didattica. In A. Barausse, T. De Freitas Ermel, & V. Viola, eds., *Prospettive incrociate sul Patrimonio Storico Educativo* (p. 271-298). Lecce: Pensa Multimedia.

Andreassi, R., & Viola, V. (2014). Percorsi per la conoscenza partecipata della Storia della Scuola: l'esperienza del Ce.S.I.S. e del Museo della scuola dell'Università degli Studi del Molise. *Glocale*(8), 231-241.

Ascenzi, A., & Brunelli, M. (2020). I musei universitari del patrimonio storico-educativo e la Terza Missione: una sfida o un'opportunità? Riflessioni dal Museo della Scuola dell'Università di Macerata. In A. Barausse, T. De Freitas Ermel, & V. Viola, eds., *Prospettive incrociate sul Patrimonio Storico Educativo* (p. 237-246). Lecce: Pensa Multimedia.

Ascenzi, A., & Patrizi, E. (2014). I Musei della scuola e dell'educazione e il patrimonio storico-educativo. Una discussione a partire dall'esperienza del Museo della scuola «Paolo e Ornella Ricca» dell'Università degli Studi di Macerata. *History of Education & Children's Literature, 9*(2), 685-714.

Ascenzi, A., Brunelli, M., & Meda, J. (2019, December 10). School museums as dynamic areas for widening the heuristic potential and the socio-cultural impact of the history of education. A case study from Italy. *Paedagogica Historica*, 1-21.

Ascenzi, A., Covato, C., & Meda, J., eds. (2020). *La pratica educativa. Storia, memoria e patrimonio.* Atti del 1° Congresso nazionale della Società Italiana per lo studio del Patrimonio Storico-Educativo (Palma de Mallorca, 20-23 novembre 2018). Macerata eum.

Ascenzi, A., Covato, C., & Zago, G., eds. (2021). *Il patrimonio storico-educativo come risorsa per il rinnovamento della didattica scolastica e universitaria: esperienze e prospettive. Atti del 2° Congresso Nazionale della Società Italiana per lo studio del Patrimonio Storico-Educativo (Padova, 7-8 ottobre 2021).* Macerata: eum.

Assemblée Nationale. (2019, mai 21). 15ème legislature. Question n. 9001: Sauvegarde du patrimoine pédagogique des anciennes écoles normales d'enseignants. Réponse. *Journal Officiel*, 4747.

Barausse, A. (2010). Alla scoperta di nuovi tesori. Le carte e i libri scolastici come beni culturali. In I. Zilli, ed., *Atlante delle emergenze culturali del Molise: risultati, riflessioni e implicazioni di un primo censimento* (p. 127-144). Campobasso: Editore Palladino.

Barausse, A. (2020). Mostre didattiche, musei pedagogici e musei scolastici in Italia dall'Unità all'ascesa del fascismo. Nation building tra processi di scolarizzazione, modernizzazione delle pratiche didattiche e relazioni transnazionali. In A. Barausse, T. De Freitas Ermel, & V. Viola, eds., *Prospettive incrociate sul Patrimonio Storico Educativo* (p. 109-150). Lecce: Pensa Multimedia.

Barausse, A., & Andreassi, R. (2019). Il Museo della scuola e dell'educazione popolare dell'Università degli Studi del Molise tra internazionalizzazione della ricerca e percorsi di educazione al patrimonio storico educativo. In V. Bosna, ed., *Itinerari nella storiografia educativa* (pp. 139-154). Bari: Cacucci.

Barausse, A., Andreassi, R., & Viola, V. (2021). La cultura scientifica e le Humanities. Catalogazione e musealizzazione dei sussidi didattici di tipo scientifico. In A. Ascenzi, C. Covato, G. Zago, eds., *Il patrimonio storico-educativo come risorsa per il rinnovamento della didattica scolastica e universitaria: esperienze e prospettive* (p. 527-550). Macerata: eum.

Barausse, A., de Freitas Ermel, T., & Viola, V., eds. (2020). *Patrimonio Storico Educativo. Atti dell'incontro Internazionale di Studi. Campobasso 2-3 Maggio 2018.* Lecce: Pensa Multimedia.

Bartolini, A. (2019). Il bene culturale e le sue plurime concezioni. *Diritto Amministrativo, 27*(2), 223-247.

Bassil, S., Crevier, Y., & Lachapelle, J. (2005). Un processus de conservation du patrimoine scolaire bâti. *Études d'histoire religieuse* (71), p. 51-64.

Becchi, E. e. (1987). *Storia dell'educazione.* Firenze: La Nuova Italia.

Belhoste, B. (2005). Culture scolaire et histoire des disciplines. *Annali di storia dell'educazione e delle istituzioni scolastiche* (12), 213-223.

Bertuccelli, L. (2017). *Insegnare e studiare la Public History da Ravenna al Master di Modena. Intervista al Professor Lorenzo Bertuccelli.* Tratto da Allacciati le storie, http://www.allacciatilestorie.it/2017/07/01/public-history-ravenna/

Bianchi, F., & Farello, P. (2010a). *Imparare a descrivere. Attività per osservare, ascoltare, confrontare, concettualizzare, definire, comprendere, produrre, esporre. Vol. 1: Scuola Primaria.* Trento: Erickson.

Bianchi, F., & Farello, P. (2010b). *Imparare a descrivere. Attività per narrare, ricordare, esporre, interpretare, responsabilizzare. Vol. 2: Scuola secondaria di primo grado.* Trento: Erickson.

Bloch, M. (1981). *Apologia della storia, o mestiere di storico.* Torino: Einaudi.

Boquet, D., & Nagy, P. (2016). Una storia diversa delle emozioni. *Rivista storica italiana, 128*(2), 472-480.

Borruso, B., Cantatore, L., & Covato, C. (2020). Il Museo della Scuola e dell'Educazione "Mauro Laeng": storia, identità e percorsi archivistici. Genesi, evoluzione e patrimonio del Museo della Scuola e dell'Educazione Mauro Laeng di Roma Tre. In J. Meda, A. Ascenzi & C. Covato, eds., *La pratica educativa. Storia, memoria e patrimonio* (p. 130-137). Macerata: eum.

Borruso, F. (2010). Su alcuni modelli educativi presenti nei quaderni scolastici dell'Archivio Didattico Lombardo Radice. In D. Montino, R. Sani & J. Meda, eds., *Exercise books. A complex source for a history of the approach to schooling and education in the 19th and 20th centuries* (p. 993-1006). Firenze: Polistampa.

Borruso, F. (2018). La scuola italiana raccontata attraverso i quaderni di scuola. L'archivio Didattico Lombardo Radice. *Il Pepe verde* (77), *Speciale MuSEd. Il museo della scuola e dell'educazione Mauro Laeng dell'Università Roma Tre* (ed. by L. Cantatore, F. Borruso), 28-31.

Borruso, F. (2019). Percorsi di una metamorfosi storiografica. Gli insegnamenti universitari e la ricerca storico-educativa italiana fra passato e presente. *Rivista di storia dell'educazione, 1,* 11-20.

Borruso, F., & Cantatore, L. (2021a). Archivio come laboratorio didattico. Il caso del fondo Lombardo Radice. In A. Ascenzi, C. Covato, G. Zago, eds., *Il patrimonio storico-educativo come risorsa per il rinnovamento della didattica scolastica e universitaria: esperienze e prospettive* (p. 447-464). Macerata: eum.

Borruso, F., & Cantatore, L. (2021b). The school notebooks collection of the Lombardo Radice Educational Archive. In J. e. Ströter-Bender, *The Children's Heritage. Provenance Research and the History of Children's and Youth Drawings Collections Museums, archives, private holding and "lost collections"* (p. 154-162). Baden-Baden: Tectum Verlag.

Borruso, F., Cantatore, L., & Covato, C. eds. (2014). *L'educazione sentimentale. Vita e norme nelle pedagogie narrate.* Milano: Guerini.

Bortolotti, A., Calidoni, M., Mascheroni, S., & Mattozzi, I. (2008). *Per l'educazione al patrimonio culturale. 22 tesi.* Milano: FrancoAngeli.

Branchesi, L., Iacono, M. R., & Riggio, A. (2019). *Educazione al patrimonio culturale in Italia e in Europa. Esperienze, modelli di riferimento, proposte per il futuro.* Roma: Italia Nostra-Media Geo.

Braster, S., Grosvenor, I., & del Pozo Andrés, M. e. (2011). *The Black Box of Schooling. A Cultural History of the Classroom.* Bruxelles [etc.]: Peter Lang.

Brighigni, D. (2010). Dalle carte dell'Archivio Diaristico Nazionale: scritture di sé nei quaderni scolastici, attraverso l'ipotesi di lettura di un diario, espressione e forma della comunicazione di massa. In J. Meda, D. Montino, & R. e. Sani, *Exercise books. A complex source for a history of the approach to schooling and education in the 19th and 20th centuries* (p. 175-186). Firenze: Polistampa.

Brunelli, M. (2013). La catalogazione dei «beni culturali» della scuola: questioni metodologiche e concettuali. In H. A. Cavallera, *La ricerca storico-educativa oggi. Un confronto di Metodi, Modelli e Programmi di ricerca, 2 vols.* (Vol. I, p. 193-218)). Lecce: Pensa Multimedia.

Brunelli, M. (2014). Las fotografías escolares como "objetos sociales". Primeras reflexiones sobre el uso educativo y social del patrimonio fotográfico en el museo de la escuela. In M. P. A.M. Badanelli Rubio, *Pedagogía museística: Prácticas, usos didácticos e investigación del patrimonio educativo. Actas de las VI Jornadas Científicas de la Sociedad Española para el Estudio del Patrimonio Histórico Educativo* (p. 203-217). Madrid: Universidad Complutense.

Brunelli, M. (2016). School Photographs. Suggestions for a Participatory Museology. In T. Stylianou-Lambert, ed.. ed., *Museums and Visitor Photography. Redefining the Visitor Experience* (p. 448-475). Edinburgh-Boston: Museums Etc.

Brunelli, M. (2017a). La recente costituzione della Società Italiana per lo studio del Patrimonio Storico-Educativo (SIPSE). *History of Education & Children's Literature, 12*(2), 653-665.

Brunelli, M. (2017b). Snapshots from the Past. School Images on the Web and the Construction of the Collective Memory of Schools. In J. Meda, M.C. Yanes-Cabrera, V. Frago, eds., *School Memories: New Trends in the History of Education* (p. 47-64). Cham: Springer International Publishing.

Brunelli, M. (2018a). Cataloghi commerciali dei materiali scolastici e collezioni storiche dei sussidi didattici: nuove fonti per la storia dell'industria per la scuola in Italia (1870-1922). *History of Education and Children's Literature»*, 13(2), 469-510.

Brunelli, M. (2018b). *L'educazione al patrimonio storico-scolastico. Approcci teorici, modelli e strumenti per la progettazione didattica e formativa in un museo della scuola.* Milano: FrancoAngeli.

Brunelli, M. (2018c). Pour une histoire de la production industrielle des matériels didactiques en Italie de la fin du XIXe à la première moitié du XXe siècle: premières indications et perspectives de recherche. In M. Figeac-Monthus, ed., *Éducation et culture matérielle en France et en Europe du XVIe siècle à nos jours* (p. 109-131). Paris: Honoré Champion.

Brunelli, M. (2020a). *Alle origini del museo scolastico: storia di un dispositivo didattico al servizio della scuola primaria e popolare tra Otto e Novecento.* Macerata: eum.

Brunelli, M. (2020b). Per una storia della circolazione dei sussidi botanici in Italia tra XIX e XX secolo. Appunti di lavoro sulle collezioni scolastiche e sui cataloghi commerciali per la scuola. In A.

Barausse, T. De Freitas Ermel, & V. Viola, eds., *Prospettive incrociate sul Patrimonio Storico Educativo* (p. 433-458). Lecce: Pensa Multimedia.

Brunelli, M. (2023). Posibles metodologías de trabajo histórico sobre la cultura material de la escuela: entre el material didáctico y los catálogos de enseñanza. In C. A. Castro, V. L. Gaspar da Silva & G. de Souza, eds., *Cultura Material Escolar em Perspectiva Histórica: Escritas e Possibilidades* (p. 246-287). São Luís: Editora da Universidade Federal do Maranhão.

Brunelli, M., & Meda, J. (2017). Gymnastics between school desks: An educational practice between hygiene requirements, health care and logistic inadequacies in Italian primary schools (1870-1970). *History of Education Review, 46*(2), 178-193.

Bruner, J. (1988). *La mente a più dimensioni.* Rome-Bari: Laterza.

Bruner, J. (2005). L'atto della scoperta. In J. Bruner, *Il conoscere. Saggi per la mano sinistra* (p. 107-124). Roma: Armando.

Buratti, N., & Ferrari, N. (2011). Introduzione. In N. Ferrari & C. Buratti, *La valorizzazione del patrimonio di prossimità tra fragilità e sviluppo locale. Un approccio multidisciplinare* (p. 9-12). Milano: Franco Angeli.

Burke, P. (2014). *Una rivoluzione storiografica.* Roma-Bari: Laterza.

Callegari, C. (2020). I filmini a immagine fissa nella scuola italiana del dopoguerra (1958-1968): un "nuovo" sussidio didattico. In A. Ascenzi, J. Meda & C. Covato, *La pratica educativa. Storia, memoria e patrimonio* (p. 345-363). Macerata: eum.

Cambi, F. (2004). La storia sociale dell'educazione: modelli e problemi. *Studi sulla formazione, 7*(1), 7-19.

Cambi, F. e. (2004). La storia sociale dell'educazione. Paradigma e modelli. *Studi sulla formazione, 7*(1), 7-172.

Cammelli, M. (2017). L'ordinamento dei beni culturali tra continuità e innovazione. *Aedon*(3), <http://www.aedon.mulino.it/archivio/2017/3/cammelli.htm> (10.12.2022).

Cammelli, M. (2020). La ratifica della convenzione di Faro: un cammino da avviare. *Aedon*(3), 186-187.

Cancellotti, C. (2011). "L'écomusée n'est pas musée". Gli ecomusei come laboratori produttori di cultura, territorio e relazione. *Altre Modernità, 5*(3), p. 99-114.

Cantatore, L. (2010). Giuseppe Lombardo Radice. Per un'idea del quaderno scolastico come fonte artistico-letteraria. In D. Montino, J. Meda & R. Sani, eds., *Exercise books. A complex source for a history of the approach to schooling and education in the 19th and 20th centuries* (p. 993-1006). Firenze: Polistampa.

Cantatore, L. (2019). The MuSEd of Roma Tre between past and present. With unpublished writings by Giuseppe Lombardo Radice and Mauro Laeng. *History of Education & Children's Literature, 14*(2), 861-884.

Cantatore, L. (2020). La vita nelle tasche di uno scolaro. In G. L. Radice, *Come si uccidono le anime, edited and introduced by L. Cantatore* (p. 7-43). Pisa: ETS.

Carpentieri, C. (2021). La Convenzione di Faro sul valore del "Cultural Heritage" per la società. Un esame giuridico. *Rivista giuridica di urbanistica, 37*(2), 274-290.

Carrattieri, M. (2020). L'Istituto nazionale per la storia del movimento di liberazione in Italia, ovvero della fase 'ingenua' della Public History. *Il capitale culturale. Studies on the Value of Cultural Heritage*(22), 51-62.

Cartei, G. F. (2007). *Convenzione europea del paesaggio e governo del territorio*. Bologna: Il Mulino.

Casini, L. (2012). Oltre la mitologia giuridica dei beni culturali. *Aedon, 1*(2), https://aedon.mulino.it/archivio/2012/1_2/casini.htm.

Casini, L. (2014). Le "parole" e le "cose": la nozione giuridica di bene culturale nella legislazione regionale. *Giornale di diritto amministrativo*(3), 257-265.

Casini, L. (2017). *Ereditare il futuro.* Bologna: Il Mulino.

Cencetti, G. (1937). Sull'archivio come "universitas rerum". *Archivi*(4), 7-13.

Certini, R. (2001). Bambini e scolari nelle memorie e nei diari di maestri e maestre: tra biografia e racconto. In S. Ulivieri & C. Covato, eds., *Itinerari nella storia dell'infanzia. Bambine e bambini, modelli pedagogici e stili educativi* (p. 197-229). Milano: Unicopli.

Chatterjee, H. e. (2008). *Touch in Museums: Policy and Practice in Object Handling.* Oxford-New York: Bloomsbury Academic.

Chatterjee, H., & Hannan, L. eds. (2015). *Engaging the Senses: Object-Based Learning in Higher Education.* Farnham-Burlington: Ashgate.

Chatterjee, H., Hannan, L., & Thomson, L. (2015). An Introduction to Object-Based Learning and Multisensory Engagement. in H. Chatterjee & L. Hannan, eds., *Engaging the Senses. Object-Based Learning in Higher Education* (p. 97-116). Farnham-Burlington: Ashgate.

Chervel, A. (1996). Des disciplines scolaires à la culture scolaire. *Paedagogica Historica*(Supplementary Series, 2), 181-195.

Chervel, A. (1998). *La culture scolaire. Une approche historique.* Paris: Bell.

Chiosso, G. (1989). *Scuola e stampa nel Risorgimento. Giornali e riviste per l'educazione prima dell'Unità.* Milano: Franco Angeli.

Chiosso, G. (1992). *I periodici scolastici nell'Italia del secondo Ottocento.* Brescia : La Scuola.

Chiosso, G. (1993). *Scuola e stampa nell'Italia liberale. Giornali e riviste per l'educazione dall'Unità a fine secolo.* Brescia: La Scuola.

Chiosso, G. (1997). *La stampa pedagogica e scolastica in Italia (1820-1943)*. Brescia: La Scuola.

Chiosso, G. (2000). *Il libro per la scuola tra Sette e Ottocento*. Brescia: La Scuola.

Chiosso, G. (2003). *TESEO: Tipografi e editori scolastico-educativi dell'Otto-cento*. Milano: Editrice Bibliografica.

Chiosso, G. (2008). *TESEO '900. Editori scolastico- educativi del primo Novecento*. Milano: Editrice Bibliografica.

Chiosso, G., & Sani, R. (2013). *Il Dizionario biografico dell'Educazione 1800-2000, 2 vols*. Milan: Editrice Bibliografica.

Civitarese Matteucci, S. (2007). Commento all'art. 131. In M. Cammelli, ed., *Il codice dei beni culturali e del paesaggio* (p. 525). Bologna: Il Mulino.

Cossetto, M. (2009). Cartelloni didattici, quadri murali, tavole parietali. In M. Cossetto & S. Spada Pintarelli, eds., *Museo della Scuo-la-Schulmuseum. Dossier. «StoriaE»*, *7(1/3)* (p. 53-54).

Covato, C. (2018). *Pericoloso a dirsi. Emozioni, sentimenti, divieti e trasgressioni*. Milano: Unicopli.

Covatta, L. (2012). *I beni culturali tra tutela, mercato e territorio*. Firenze: Passigli.

D'Acquisto, L. (2006). *Learning on Display: Student-Created Museums that Build Understanding*. Alexandria: Association for Supervision and Curriculum Development.

D'Acquisto, L. (2013). Museums at School. *Educational Leadership, 70*(5), https://ascd.org/el/articles/museums-at-school.

D'Alessio, M. (2014). Dentro la vita della scuola. Per una riflessione sulle nuove fonti di studio del patrimonio storico-educativo. *Bollettino Storico della Basilicata*(30), 171-185.

D'Alessio, M. (2014). Life at school: class registers as a new source of studying historical and educational heritage. In A.M.a Badanelli Rubio, M. Poveda Sanz & C. Rodríguez Guerrero, eds., *Pedagogia museística: Prácticas, usos didácticos e investigación del patrimonio educativo* (p. 401-409). Madrid: Universidad Complutense-MCF Textos.

D'Alessio, M. (2020, July-September). Per la salvaguardia del patrimonio scolastico-educativo al tempo del Covid-19. *L'eco della scuola nuova. Organo della FNISM Federazione Nazionale Insegnanti»*, 75(3), 3.

D'Alessio, M., & Tomasco, C. (2021). In A. Ascenzi, C. Covato, G. Zago, *Il patrimonio storico-educativo come risorsa per il rinnovamento della didattica scolastica e universitaria. Esperienze e prospettive* (p. 79-92). Macerata: eum.

D'Ascenzo, M. (1997). *La scuola elementare in età liberale. Il caso Bologna, 1859-1911*. Bologna: Clueb.

D'Ascenzo, M. (2008). *Scuola, didattica e musei tra Otto e Novecento: il Museo didattico "Luigi Bombicci" di Bologna*. Bologna: Clueb.

D'Ascenzo, M. (2014). A didactic instrument of historical and educational interest: The case of the Luigi Bombicci Scientific Didactic Museum. In A.M. a Badanelli Rubio, M. Poveda Sanz & C. Rodríguez Guerrero, eds., Pedagogía museística. *Prácticas, usos didácticos investigación del patrimonio educativo* (p. 411-419). Madrid: Universidad complutense de Madrid-MCF Textos.

D'Ascenzo, M. (2019). Esperienze di 'Public History of Education' nell'Università di Bologna, tra ricerca scientifica e didattica. In G. Bandini, S. Oliviero, edds., *Public History of Education: riflessioni, testimonianze, esperienze* (p. 211-221). Firenze: FUP.

D'Ascenzo, M. (2020). I musei didattici tra Ottocento e Novecento in Italia come fonti per la storia della scuola e patrimonio storico educativo. In A. Ascenzi, C. Covato, & J. Meda, *La pratica educativa. Storia, memoria e patrimonio* (p. 171-189). Macerata: eum.

De Berti, R. (2004). L'istituzionalizzazione del cinematografo nei manuali Hoepli (1907-1923). *Comunicazioni sociali*(1), [1-8].

De Fort, E. (2002). Storie di scuole, storia della scuola: sviluppi e tendenze della storiografia. In M.T. Sega, *La scuola fa la storia. Gli archivi scolastici per la ricerca e la didattica* (p. 31-70). Portogruaro: Nuova Dimensione.

De Giorgi, F. (2014). Appunti sulla storia del banco scolastico. *Rivista di storia dell'educazione*(1), 85-98.

De Varine, H. (2005a). *Le radici del futuro. Il patrimonio culturale al servizio dello sviluppo locale.* Ed. by D. Jalla. Bologna: Clueb.

De Varine, H. (2005b). L'ecomuseo. In *Le radici del futuro. Il patrimonio culturale al servizio dello sviluppo locale* (p. 241-273). Bologna: Clueb.

De Varine, H. (2005c). Uno strumento per lo sviluppo: il museo scolastico. In H. De Varine, *Le radici del futuro. Il patrimonio culturale al servizio dello sviluppo locale* (p. 144-177). Bologna: Clueb.

Demetrio, D. (2004). *Ricordare a scuola. Fare memoria didattica e autobiografia.* Roma, Bari: Laterza.

Depaepe, M., & Simon, F. (1995). Is there any Place for the History of 'Education' in the 'History of Education'? A plea for the History of Everyday Educational Reality in-and outside Schools. *Paedagogica historica, 30*(1), 9-16.

Desvallées, A., & Mairesse, F. (2010). *Key Concepts of Museology.* Paris: A. Colin-ICOM.

Di Biasio, S., & Gargano, T. (2021). Da "sedere compostamente" a "stare comodamente": l'esperienza delle scuole dell'Agro romano e pontino come laboratorio sulla storia del banco scolastico. In A. Ascenzi, C. Covato, G. Zago, eds., *Il patrimonio storico-educativo come risorsa per il rinnovamento della didattica scolastica e universi-taria. Esperienze e prospettive* (p. 465-478). Macerata: eum.

Di Vaio, F. (2014). *Mostra delle scuole storiche napoletane: archivi, biblioteche, gabinetti scientifici, cimeli, patrimonio storico-artistico e architetton-ico (Archivio di Stato di Napoli, 2 aprile-30 maggio 2014). Catalogo.* Napoli: Giannini.

Di Vaio, F. (2017). *La Grande Guerra. Testimonianze nelle Scuole Storiche Napoletane. Mostra documentaria: lapidi, monumenti, cimeli, opuscoli commemorativi, annuari (Università Suor Orsola Benincasa, 13-28 ottobre 2016). Catalogo.* Napoli: Giannini.

D'Alessio, M. (2020). «La Memoria e le carte. Gli archivi e la valoriz-zazione del patrimonio storico- educativo». A proposito del Convegno nazionale di studi (Matera, 4 e 5 ottobre 2019). *History of Education & Children's Literature, 15*(1), 791-807.

Dierking, L. (2002). The Role of Context in Children's Learning From Objects and Experiences. In S. Paris, ed., *Perspectives on Object-Centered Learning in Museums* (p. 3-18). Mahwah-London: Laurence Erlbaum Associates.

Dudley, S. H. (2010). *Museum Materialities: Objects, Engagements, Interpre-tations.* London and New York: Routledge.

Dudley, S. H. (2012). *Museum Objects. Experiencing the Properties of Things.* London-New York: Routledge.

Durbin, G., Morris, S., & Wilkinson, S. (1990). *Learning from Objects. A Teacher's guide.* London: English Heritage.

Elia, D. F. (2012). Giuseppe Pezzarossa's (1880-1911) gymnastics equip-ment workshop. *History of Education & Children's Literature, 7*(1), 469-488.

Elia, D. F. (2016). Ginnastica e mezzi di educazione di massa: Pietro Gallo e l'introduzione del bastone Jäger in Italia (1878). In *Atti del Convegno di Studi Cirse "Sguardi della storia. Luoghi, figure, immaginario e teorie dell'educazione"* (p. CD-Rom attached to "Rivista di Storia dell'Educazione", 3/2.). Firenze: FUP.

Elia, D. F. (2017). Per una promozione dei mezzi di educazione di massa nella ginnastica: l'opera di Pietro Gallo (1841-1916). *History of Education & Children's Literature, 12*(1), 507-525.

Elia, D. F. (2021). Le palestre italiane nell'Ottocento: modelli regionali a confronto. *Studi sulla Formazione, 24*(1), 127-144.

Escolano Benito, A. (2005). Etnohistoria e historia de la escuela. *Annali di storia dell'educazione e delle istituzioni scolastiche*(12), 197-206.

Escolano Benito, A. (2007). *La cultura material de la escuela.* Berlanga de Duero: CEINCE.

Etnohistoria de la escuela. XII Coloquio Nacional de Historia de la Educación (Burgos, 18-21 junio 2003). (2003). Burgos: Sociedad Española de Historia de la Educación-Junta de Castilla y León, Consejería de Educación y Cultura-Universidad de Burgos.

European Commission. (2018). Council Recommendation of 22 May 2018 on key competences for lifelong learning. *Official Journal of the European Union*, https://data.europa.eu/doi/10.2766/569540.

Farge, A. (2003). *Il braccialetto di pergamena. Lo scritto su di sé nel XVIII secolo.* Milano: Edizioni Sylvestre Bonnard.

Farnè, R. (1998). Giocattoli e educazione. *Encyclopaideia, 2*(2), 117-139.

Feliciati, P. (2015). La valorizzazione dell'eredità culturale in Italia. *Il capitale culturale. Studies on the Value of Cultural Heritage*(Supplement 5).

Ferrari, M., & Morandi, M. (2017). *Le cose e le loro lezioni. Itinerari di analisi pedagogica in prospettiva diacronica.* Mantova: Municipality of Mantova.

Ferrari, M., Morandi, M., & E. Platé, E. (2008). *La lezione delle cose: oggetti didattici delle scuole dell'infanzia mantovane tra Ottocento e Novecento.* Mantova: PubliPaolini-Municipality of Mantova.

Ferrari, M., Morandi, M., & Platé, E. (2011). *Lezioni di cose, lezioni di immagini. Studi di caso e percorsi di riflessione sulla scuola italiana tra XIX e XXI secolo.* Parma: Spaggiari-Edizioni Junior.

Ferrari, M., Panizza, G., & Morandi, M. (2008). I beni culturali della scuola: conservazione e valorizzazione . *Annali di storia dell'educazione e delle istituzioni scolastiche, 15,* Monographic section, pp. 15-191.

Fogliardi, G., & Marcadella, G. (2010). *Gli archivi ispirano la scuola. Fonti d'archivio per la didattica. Atti del convegno di studi Trento (21 novembre 2008).* Roma: Ministry of Tourism and Cultural Heritage and Activities.

Frondizi, R. (2020). *La terza missione dell'Università. Strategia, valutazione e performance.* Milano: Giappichelli.

Galeffi, A., & Sardo, L. (2021). Comunicare la catalogazione: un'indagine sulle aspettative degli studenti e sulle esigenze professionali, *AIB Studi, 61*(1, January-April), p. 31-53.

Gardner, H. (2013). *Formae mentis. Saggio sulla pluralità dell'intelligenza.* Milano: Feltrinelli.

Gardner, H. (2022). Il concetto di intelligenze multiple vent'anni dopo. In H. Gardner, *Educazione e sviluppo della mente. Intelligenze multiple e apprendimento* (p. 77-86). Trento: Erickson.

Garnett, A. (2010, September 18). *Improving object descriptions in UCL's Object-Based Learning Lab.* In: Culture Blog: https://blogs.ucl.ac.uk/museums/2020/09/28/improving-object-descriptions-in-ucls-object-based-learning-lab/

Gaspar da Silva, V., Meda, M., & de Souza, G. (2021). The material turn in the History of Education. *Educació i història*(38), 1-176.

Genovesi, G. (2008). *Il quaderno umile segno di scuola.* Milano: Franco Angeli.

Gianini Belotti, E. (1973). *Dalla parte delle bambine.* Milano: Feltrinelli.

Gibelli, A. (2012). Bambini e bambine alle prese con la scrittura: uno
    sguardo storico sul secolo XX. *History of Education & Children's
    Literature*, 7(1), 183-199.

Gibson, J. (1999). *Un approccio ecologico alla percezione visiva* . Bologna: Il
    Mulino.

Ginzburg, C. (1992). *Miti, emblemi, spie. Morfologia e storia*. Torino:
    Einaudi.

Ginzburg, C. (2000). *Rapporti di forza: storia, retorica, prova*. Milano: Feltr-
    inelli.

Giorgi, P. (2011). La fotografia nella scuola. In *Alle radici dell'identità nazi-
    onale: Italia Nazione culturale* (p. 213-224). Roma: Gangemi.

Giorgi, P. (2016). Sviluppi dell'edilizia scolastica in Italia (XIX-XX
    secolo). In G. Biondi, S. Borri, & L. Tosi, eds., *Dall'aula all'ambi-
    ente di apprendimento* (p. 109-127). Firenze: Altralinea Edizioni.

Giorgi, P. (2021). Indagine su una raccolta di elaborati scolastici: oggetto
    misterioso per un laboratorio didattico. Il progetto 'Il laborato-
    rio di storia' lo studente come lo storico alla ricerca delle fonti.
    In A. Ascenzi, C. Covato, & G. Zago, eds., *Il patrimonio storico-ed-
    ucativo e il rinnovamento della didattica universitaria e scolastica:
    riflessioni teoriche e metodologiche* (p. 623-634). Macerata: eum.

Giorgi, P., & Franchi, E. (2012). *L'obiettivo sulla scuola. Immagini dall'ar-
    chivio fotografico INDIRE*. Firenze: Giunti.

Gobierno de Cantabria. (2005, julio 1). Decreto del Consejo n. 71/2005
    de 23 de junio. *Boletín Oficial de Cantabria*, 7(1), 1 de julio 2005:
    http://www.muesca.es/.

Gobierno de Cantabria. (2014, diciembre 23). Resolución de 15 de
    diciembre de 2014 que establece las condiciones para la gestión
    del patrimonio histórico educativo de los centros docentes de
    la Consejeria de Educacion, Cultura y Deporte del Gobierno de
    Cantabria. *Boletín Oficial de Cantabria*(246), 38269-38275.

Grosvenor, I., Lawn, M., & Rousmaniere, K. (1999). *Silences and Images. The Social History of the Classroom.* New York: Peter Lang.

Gualdani, A. (2020). L'Italia ratifica la convenzione di Faro: quale incidenza nel diritto del patrimonio culturale italiano? *Aedon*(3), 272-280.

Guerra, M. (2022). *Le più piccole cose. L'esplorazione come esperienza educativa.* Milano: Franco Angeli.

Hawkins, D. (1979). Pasticciando con le scienze (1965). In D. Hawkins, *Imparare a vedere. Saggi sull'apprendimento e sulla natura umana* (p. 84-94). Torino: Loescher.

Hébrard, J. (1995). Lo spazio grafico del quaderno scolastico in Francia tra Otto e Novecento. In In Q. Antonelli, & E. Becchi, eds., *Scritture bambine* (p. 145-175). Roma-Bari: Laterza.

Hernández Huerta, J. L., Payà Rico, A., & Grau Vidal, R. (2021). La revista Cabás y la SEPHE como órganos de difusión del conocimiento histórico-educativo. *Cabás*(26), 139-152.

Hooper Greenhill, E. (1992). *Museums and the Shaping of Knowledge.* London-New York: Routledge.

Hooper Greenhill, E. (1999). *The Educational Role of Museums, 2nd ed.* London: Routledge.

I quaderni di scuola tra Otto e Novecento. (2006). Annali di storia dell'educazione e delle istituzioni scolastiche. *I quaderni di scuola tra Otto e Novecento. Monographic section*(13), 11-189.

Ibrayeva, A., Kalkeyeva, K., Khamitovna, U., & Sanakulova, B. (2015). Conceptual basis of the creation of the Museum of National Education History. *Review of European Studies, 7*(6), 194-200.

Jalla, D. (2009). *Per un museo scolastico diffuso.* In: Museiscuola, <http://www.comune.torino.it/museiscuola/partecipa/approfondimenti/per-un-museo-scolastico-diffuso.shtml>

Jalla, D., Lonjon, C., Pizzigoni, F., & Vuillet, T. (2011). *L'École est notre Patrimoine/La Scuola è il nostro Patrimonio*. Torino: Tip. Sosso.

Julia, D. (1995a). La culture scolaire comme objet historique. In A. Nóvoa, M. Depaepe, & E. Johanningmeier, *The Colonial Experience in Education: Historical Issues and Perspectives* (Vol. «Paedagogica Historica», Supplementary Series, I, 1995, p. 353-382).

Julia, D. (1995b). La cultura escolar come objeto histórico. In M. Menegus, & E. González, *Historia de las Universidades modernas en Hispanoamérica: métodos y fuentes* (p. 131-153). Mexico: Universidad Nacional Autónoma de México.

Julia, D. (1996). Riflessioni sulla recente storiografia dell'educazione in Europa: per una storia comparata delle culture scolastiche. *Annali di storia dell'educazione e delle istituzioni scolastiche*, 3(3), 119-147.

Julia, D. (1996). Riflessioni sulla recente storiografia dell'educazione in Europa: per una storia comparata delle culture scolastiche. *Annali di storia dell'educazione e delle istituzioni scolastiche*(3), 119-147.

Julia, D., Pazzaglia, L., Betti, C., & Tognon, G. (2004). La storia dell'educazione come storia culturale. *Contemporanea*, 7(2), 263-286.

Lane, J., & Wallace, A. (2011). *Hands On: Learning from Objects and Paintings. A Teacher's Guide*. Glasgow: Scottish Museums Council, .

Leinhardt, G., & Crowley, K. (2002). Objects of Learning, Objects of Talk: Changing Minds in Museums. In S. Paris, *Perspectives on Object-Centered Learning in Museums* (p. 301-324). Mahwah-London: Lawrence Erlbaum Associates.

Lejeune, P. (1975). *Il patto autobiografico*. Bologna: Il Mulino.

Lombardi, L. (2010). Il metodo visivo in Italia: le proiezioni luminose nella scuola elementare italiana (1908-1930). *History of Education & Children's Literature*, 5(2), 1000-1024.

Lombardi, M. (2007). Authentic learning for the 21st century: An overview. *EDUCAUSE Learning Initiative*, 1, 1-12.

Lombardo Radice, G. (1925). *Athena fanciulla. Scienza e poesia della scuola serena.* Firenze: Bemporad.

Macchietti, S. S. (1990). *Problemi e prospettive della ricerca storico-pedagogica.* Roma: Bulzoni.

Malaguzzi, L., & Gandini, L. (2017). La storia, le idee e la cultura: la voce e il pensiero di Loris Malaguzzi. Intervista di Lella Gandini. In C. Edwards, L. Gandini, & G. Forman, *I cento linguaggi dei bambini. L'approccio di Reggio Emilia all'educazione dell'infanzia* (p. 55-111). Bergamo: Edizioni Junior.

Mancinelli, M. L. (2017). *Normativa Trasversale versione 4.00 - Strutturazione dei dati e Norme di compilazione.* Roma: ICCD-Ministry of Tourism and Cultural Heritage and Activities.

Mancinelli, M. L. (2018). Gli standard catalografici dell'Istituto Centrale per il Catalogo e la Documentazione. In R. Tucci, *Le voci, le opere e le cose. La catalogazione dei beni culturali demoetnoantropologici* (p. 279-302). Roma: ICCD-Ministry of Tourism and Cultural Heritage and Activities.

Marcarini, M. (2016). *Pedarchitettura. Linee storiche ed esempi attuali in Italia e in Europa.* Roma: Studium.

Marchis, V. e. (2014). *Strumentaria e modellistica didattica nelle scuole secondarie dell'area metropolitana torinese.* Torino: Politecnico .

Marrone, L., & Molisso, G. (2011). Insegnare la scienza dei Greci: un'esperienza didattica interdisciplinare. *AION: Annals from the University of Naples L'Orientale*, p. 187-206.

Mazzei, L., & Alovisio, S. (2016, November 10). Vedere lontano: cinema ed educazione alla geografia nell'Italia degli anni Dieci. *Cinergie*, 27-43.

Meda, J. (2006a). La politica quotidiana. L'utilizzo propagandistico del diario scolastico nella scuola fascista. *History of Education & Children's Literature, 1*(1), 287-313.

Meda, J. (2006b). Quaderni di scuola. Nuove fonti per la storia dell'editoria scolastica minore. *Annali di storia dell'educazione e delle istituzioni scolastiche in Italia*(13), 73-98.

Meda, J. (2007). Sgorbi e scarabocchi. Guida ragionata alle collezioni storiche di disegni infantili. *History of Education & Children's Literature, 2*(1), 349-350.

Meda, J. (2010). Musei della scuola e dell'educazione. Ipotesi progettuale per una sistematizzazione delle iniziative di raccolta, conservazione e valorizzazione dei beni culturali delle scuole. *History of Education & Children's Literature, 5*(2), p. 489-501.

Meda, J. (2013). La conservazione del patrimonio storico educativo: il caso italiano. In A. M. Badanelli, & J. Meda, *La historia de la cultura escolar en Italia y en España: balance y perspectivas: actas del 1° Workshop Italo-Español de Historia de la cultura escolar in Italia y en Espana: balance y perspectivas* (p. 167-198). Macerata: eum.

Meda, J. (2016a). Dalla disciplina al design. L'evoluzione del banco scolastico in Italia tra Ottocento e Novecento. In G. Biondi, S. Borri & L. Tosi, eds., *Dall'aula all'ambiente di apprendimento* (p. 129-150). Firenze: AltraLinea Edizioni.

Meda, J. (2016b). *Mezzi di educazione di massa. Saggi di storia della cultura materiale della scuola tra XIX e XX secolo.* Milano: Franco Angeli.

Meda, J. (2019). Il patrimonio storico-educativo: oggetti da museo o fonti materiali per una nuova storia dell'educazione? In V. Bosna (ed.), *Itinerari nella storiografia educativa* (p. 139-154). Bari: Cacucci Editore.

Meda, J. (2022). Un esperimento didattico di alternativa ai libri di testo nella scuola fascista: il Manifesto scolastico settimanale (1934-1937). In A. Ascenzi & R. Sani, eds., *L'innovazione pedagogica e didattica nel sistema formativo italiano dall'Unità al secondo dopoguerra* (p. 195-226). Roma: Studium.

Meda, J., & Polenghi, S. (2021). From educational theories to school materialities: The genesis of the material history of school in Italy (1990-2020). *Educació i història*(38), 55-77.

Meda, J., Cabrera, C., & Viñao, A., eds. (2017). *School Memories. New Trends in the History of Education.* Cham: Springer.

Meda, J., Montino, D., & Sani, R., eds. (2010). *Exercise books. A Complex Source for a History of the Approach to Schooling and Education in the 19th and 20th Centuries, 2 vols.* Firenze: Polistampa.

MIBACT. (2009). *Catalogo dei beni culturali architettonici. Edifici scolastici.* Torino: Ministry of Cultural Heritage and Activities-Municipality of Turin.

Mieussens, M., & Bouhier, C. (2017). Un réseau qui dit s'organiser: les 170 musées de l'école en France. In A. Hurel, ed., *La France Savante. Actes du 140e Congrès national des sociétés historiques et scientifiques* (p. 366-379). Paris: Editions du Comité des travaux historiques et scientifiques.

Molisso, G. (2019). *Il progetto NEMO: un museo scientifico diffuso.* Napoli: Artem-NEMO.

Molisso, G. (2021a). Un'esperienza didattica con l'apparecchio di Hope del Museo di fisica del Liceo "Vittorio Emanuele II" di Napoli. In A. Ascenzi, C. Covato, & G. Zago, eds., *Il patrimonio storico-educativo come risorsa per il rinnovamento della didattica scolastica e universitaria: esperienze e prospettive* (p. 651-658). Macerata: eum.

Molisso, G. (2021b). Un percorso di PCTO nel Museo del Liceo "Vittorio Emanuele II" di Napoli. In A. Ascenzi, C. Covato, G. Zago, eds., *Il patrimonio storico-educativo come risorsa per il rinnovamento della didattica scolastica e universitaria: esperienze e prospettive* (p. 645-650). Macerata: eum.

Molisso, G., & Cavaliere, M. R. (2019). Il Progetto NEMO In G. Molisso, *Il progetto NEMO Un museo scientifico diffuso.* Napoli: Artem-NEMO

Monopoli, R. (2012). *Museum of "La Defizia" School.* In: Puglia Digital Library: <http://www.pugliadigitallibrary.it/item. jsp?id=3361&locale=it_IT>

Montessori, M. (2018). *La scoperta del bambino (1948).* Milano: RCS MediaGroup.

Montino, D. (2005). *Le parole educate. Libri e quaderni tra fascismo e Repubblica.* Milano: Selene.

Montino, D. (2006). Quaderni scolastici e costruzione dell'immaginario infantile minore. *Annali dell'educazione*(13), 167-189.

Neri, R. (1977). *Educazione infantile: gioco e giocattoli.* Roma: Lucarini.

Noiret, S. (2015). Storia pubblica digitale. *Zapruder. Storie in movimento*(36), 9-23.

Novara, D. (2018). *Cambiare la scuola si può. Un nuovo metodo per insegnanti e genitori, per un'educazione finalmente efficace.* Milano: BUR.

Ortolano, F., & Treccarichi, F. (2021). Museiscuol@: sostenere un heritage community. In A. Ascenzi, C. Covato, & G. Zago, eds., *Il patrimonio storico-educativo come risorsa per il rinnovamento della didattica scolastica e universitaria. Esperienze e prospettive* (pp. 659-676). Macerata: eum.

Paciaroni, L. (2020). *Memorie di scuola. Contributo a una storia delle pratiche didattiche ed educative nelle scuole marchigiane attraverso le testimonianze di maestri e maestre (1945-1985).* Macerata: eum.

Paris, S., ed. (2002). *Perspectives on Object-Centered Learning in Museums.* Mahwah-London: Lawrence Erlbaum Associates.

Periotto, D., Pizzigoni, F. D., & Treccarichi, F. (2021). Tra formazione comune e progettualità condivisa: la Rete dei Musei scolastici torinesi. In A. Ascenzi, C. Covato, & G. Zago, eds., *Il patrimonio storico-educativo come risorsa per il rinnovamento della didattica scolastica e universitaria. Esperienze e prospettive* (pp. 717-730). Macerata: eum.

Pizzigoni, F. D. (2012). The pedagogic museums as a tool for historiographical research. *History of Education & Children's Literature, 7*(2), 557-577.

Pizzigoni, F. D. (2013). *Bambini al museo o il museo a scuola? Il museo scolastico come strumento di didattica attiva: l'esempio della scuola XXV Aprile di Torino.* <http://www.comune.torino.it/museiscuola/bm~doc/rivista-infanzia_art-di-pizzigoni.pdf>

Pizzigoni, F. D. (2015). Imparare a imparare attraverso il museo scolastico: tracce di nuove potenzialità di uno strumento didattico tardo-ottocentesco. *Form@re, 15*(3), 142-158.

Pizzigoni, F. D. (2016). Del patrimonio de una escuela al patrimonio de todas: reflexiones sobre el catálogo virtual de los museos escolares de Turín. In P. Dávila, & L. M.a Naya, eds., *Espacios y patrimonio histórico-educativo: VII Jornadas Científicas de la SEPHE y V Simposio Iberoamericano* (pp. 1199-1210). Donostia: Erein.

Pizzigoni, F. D. (2019). The Beckwith school-museums as a place of memory. *History of Education & Children's Literature, 14*(1), 91-107.

Pizzigoni, F. D. (2020). L'armadio-museo: un alleato per la didattica nella pluriclasse, ieri e oggi. *Formazione & Insegnamento, 18*(1), 17- 29.

Pizzigoni, F. D. (2021). Realizzare il museo scolastico attraverso un percorso attivo e partecipativo: il "Patrimoniere". In A. Ascenzi, C. Covato, & G. Zago, eds., *Il patrimonio storico-educativo come risorsa per il rinnovamento della didattica scolastica e universitaria: esperienze e prospettive.* (p. 195-210). Macerata: eum.

Pizzigoni, F. D. (2022a). *Il metodo del "Patrimoniere": il patrimonio scolastico per rafforzare l'identità e superare l'isolamento.* Firenze: Indire-I Quaderni delle piccole scuole, n. 9.1.

Pizzigoni, F. D. (2022b). *Tracce di patrimonio. Fonti per lo studio del patri-monio scolastico ed educativo nell'Italia del secondo Ottocento.* Lecce: Pensa Multimedia.

Pizzigoni, F. D. (2022c). El uso educativo del patrimonio histórico y las teorías del aprendizaje: una relación a destacar. *CABÁS*(22), 239-256.

Popkewitz, T. S., Franklin, B. M., & Pereyra, M. A. (2001). *Cultural History and Education: Critical Essays on Knowledge and Schooling.* New York-London: Routledge Falmer.

Portelli, A. (2017). *Storie orali. Racconti, immaginazione, dialogo.* Roma: Donzelli.

Predieri, A. (1969). Significato della norma costituzionale sulla tutela del paesaggio. In *Studi per il XX Anniversario dell'Assemblea costit-uente. Vol. II: Le libertà civili e politiche* (pp. 381-428). Firenze: Vallecchi.

Pruneri, F. (2006). *Oltre l'alfabeto. L'istruzione popolare dall'Unità d'Italia all'età giolittiana: il caso di Brescia.* Milano: Vita e Pensiero.

Pruneri, F. (2014). L'aula scolastica tra Otto e Novecento. *Rivista di storia dell'educazione*(1), 63-72.

Ragazzini, D. (1983). *Storia della scuola italiana. Linee generali e problemi di ricerca.* Firenze: Le Monnier.

Raicich, M. (1982). *Scuola, cultura e politica da De Sanctis a Gentile.* Pisa: Nistri-Lischi.

Ridolfi, M. (2017). *Verso la Public History. Fare e raccontare storia nel tempo presente.* Pisa: Pacini.

Rizzolatti, G., & Sinigaglia, C. (2006). *So quel che fai. Il cervello che agisce e i neuroni specchio.* Milano: Raffaello Cortina Editore.

Rocard, M., ed. (2007). *Science Education NOW: A Renewed Pedagogy for the Future of Europe.* Brussels: European Commission.

Ruiz Berrio, J. ed. (2000). *La cultura escolar de Europa. Tendencias históricas emergentes.* Madrid: Editorial Bibliotea Nueva.

Sani, R. (2011). *"Sub specie educationis". Studi e ricerche su istruzione, istituzioni scolastiche e processi culturali e formativi nell'Italia contemporanea.* Macerata: eum.

Sani, R. (2012). Exercise books as a source of the history of education and cultural processes. Toward an on-going assessment of studies conducted in Italy over the last decade. *History of Education & Children's Literature, 7*(2), 477-496.

Sani, R. (2013). Bilancio della ricerca sui quaderni scolastici in Italia. In J. Meda, & A. Badanelli, eds., *La historia de la cultura escolar en Italia y en España: balance y perspectivas* (pp. 83-103). Macerata: eum.

Sani, R. (2016). *Storia dell'educazione e delle istituzioni scolastiche nell'Italia moderna.* Milano: Franco Angeli.

Sani, R. (2018). L'implementazione della ricerca sul patrimonio storico-educativo in Italia: itinerari, priorità, obiettivi di lungo termine. In S. González, J. Meda, X. Motilla & L. Pomante, eds., *La práctica educativa. Historia, Memoria y Patrimonio. Atti delle VII Jornadas Científicas de la SEPHE - I Congresso Nazionale della SIPSE (Palma de Mallorca, 20-23 November 2018)* (pp. 27-44). Salamanca: FarenHouse.

Sani, R. (2019). La ricerca sul patrimonio storico-educativo in Italia. *Revista Linhas, 20* (44), 53-74.

Sani, R., & Meda, J. (2022). «School Memories between Social Perception and Collective Representation». Un progetto di ricerca innovativo e a marcata vocazione internazionale. *History of Education & Children's Literature, 17* (1), 9-26.

Santamaita, S. (2013). *Storia dell'educazione e delle pedagogie.* Milano: Bruno Mondadori Università.

Santoni Rugiu, A., & Trebisacce, G., eds. (1983). *I problemi epistemologici e metodologici della ricerca storico/educativa.* Cosenza: Pellegrini.

Sanzo, A. (2020). *A. Sanzo, Storia del Museo d'Istruzione e di Educazione. Tessera dopo tessera.* Roma: Anicia.

Scapellato, B. (2017). *Inquiry-Based Science Education. Dalla teoria alla pratica: l'approccio IBSE per una comprensione profonda delle scienze naturali.* Torino: Pearson.

Scardamalia, M., & Bereiter, C. (2006). Knowledge building: Theory, pedagogy, and technology. In R. K. Sawyer, ed., *The Cambridge Handbook of the Learning Sciences* (pp. 97-118). New York: Cambridge University Press.

Sciullo, G. (2020). Patrimonio e beni. In C. Barbati, M. Cammelli, L. Casini, G. Piperata & G. Sciullo, eds., *Diritto del patrimonio culturale* (pp. 37-72). Bologna: Il Mulino.

Scovazzi, T., Ubertazzi, B., & Zagato, L., eds. (2012). *Il patrimonio culturale intangibile nelle sue diverse dimensioni.* Milano: Giuffrè.

Sénat Française. (2019, décembre 12). 15e Législature. Question n. 11876: Sauvegarde du patrimoine pédagogique des établissements scolaires. Réponse. *Journal Officiel*, 6143.

Singh, S. (2017). *The Educational Heritage of Ancient India: How an Ecosystem of Learning Was Laid to Waste.* Chennai: Notion Press.

Singh, S. (2022). *Revisiting the Educational Heritage of India.* Bryn Mawr: Global Collective Publishers.

Spampani, G. (2016). Material history of the school. Evolution and changes of the classroom in Italy. In P. Dávila & L. M.a Naya, eds., *Espacios y patrimonio histórico-educativo* (pp. 366-367). Donostia: Erein.

Taillefait, A. (2002). *Gestion du patrimoine scolaire: bâtiments et mobilier.* Boulogne-Billancourt: Berger-Levrault.

Tarasco, A. (2004). *Beni patrimonio e attività culturali: attori privati e autonomie territoriali.* Napoli: Editoriale Scientifica.

Targhetta, F. (2015). Teaching with Images Between 19th and 20th Centuries: The Case of the Italian School Publisher Paravia. *Strenæ. Recherches sur les livres et objets culturels de l'enfance* (8), https://journals.openedition.org/strenae/1392.

Targhetta, F. (2020). Una fonte preziosa per gli studi storico educativi: film e filmine didattiche. In A. Barausse, T. De Freitas Ermel, & V. Viola, eds., *Prospettive incrociate sul Patrimonio Storico Educativo* (pp. 459-469). Lecce: Pensa Multimedia.

Targhetta, F. (2022). La rivoluzione delle immagini: quadri murali e proiezioni luminose tra '800 e '900. In R. Sani & A. Ascenzi, eds., *L'innovazione pedagogica e didattica nel sistema formativo italiano dall'Unità al secondo dopoguerra* (pp. 266-278). Roma: Studium edizioni.

Tiballi, A. (2015). Engaging the Past: Haptics and Object-Based Learning in multiple Dimensions. In H. J. Chatterjee & L. Hannan, eds., *Engaging the Senses. Object-Based Learning in Higher Education* (pp. 57-75). Farnham-Burlington: Ashgate.

Tucci, R. (2017). *Normativa BDM - Beni Demoetnoantropologici Materiali versione 4.00 - Strutturazione dei dati e norme di compilazione.* Roma: ICCD-Ministry of Tourism and Cultural Heritage and Activities.

Ulivieri, S. (2015). La componente storica del sapere pedagogico. La ricerca storico-educativa oggi. Tendenze storiografiche e linee di ricerca. In G. Elia, ed., *La complessità del sapere pedagogico tra tradizione e innovazione* (pp. 15-28). Milano: Franco Angeli .

Vanni, L. (2015). Tra banchi, quaderni e calamai: la storia materiale della scuola nelle immagini della Fototeca storica INDIRE. *Studi sulla formazione* (2), 209-224.

Vasco Rocca, S. (2003). *Beni culturali e catalogazione. Principi teorici e percorsi di analisi.* Roma: Gangemi.

Vidal, D. (2020). *Sujeitos e artefatos: territórios de uma história transnacional da educação.* Belo Horizonte: Fino Traço.

Viñao Frago, A. (1998). Por una historia de la cultura escolar: enfoques, cuestiones, fuentes. In *Culturas y civilizaciones. III Congreso de la Asociación de Historia Contemporánea* (pp. 167-183). Valladolid: Universidad de Valladolid.

Viñao Frago, A. (2012). La historia material e inmaterial de la escuela: memoria, patrimonio y educación. *Educação, 35* (1), 7-17.

Viola, V. (2014). Cataloguing school cultural heritage. The experience of University of studies of Molise. In A. M. Badanelli Rubio, M. Poveda Sanz & C. Rodriguez Guerrero, eds., *Pedagogía museística: práticas, usos didácticos e investigación del patrimonio educativo". Actas de las VI Jornada científicas de la SEPHE* (pp. 153-162). Madrid: Universidad Complutense.

Viola, V. (2016). "The school house". History and evolution of the urban and rural school building in Italy during the fascism. In P. Davila & L. M.a Naya, eds., *Espacios y patrimonio histórico-educativo* (pp. 377-389). Donostia: Erein.

Viola, V. (2018a). Processi di scolarizzazione e spazi rurali: l'edilizia scolastica per le scuole rurali. In M. D'Alessio & A. Barausse, eds., *Processi di scolarizzazione e paesaggio rurale in Italia tra Otto e Novecento. Itinerari ed esperienze tra oblio, rappresentazione, propaganda e realtà* (pp. 65-92). Lecce: Pensa Multimedia.

Viola, V. (2018b). Gli spazi della memoria scolastica. Prime riflessioni sugli edifici scolastici come luoghi di apprendimento e monumenti attraverso un excursus storico dall'Unità d'Italia alla caduta del fascismo. In: S. González, J. Meda, X. Motilla & L. Pomante, eds., *La práctica educativa. Historia, Memoria y Patrimonio.* (pp. 251-264). Salamanca: FahrenHouse.

Viola, V. (2019). L'edilizia scolastica in Italia ai tempi del fascismo. *História da Educação* (23), https://doi.org/10.1590/2236-3459/82782.

Vitale, C. (2010). La fruizione dei beni culturali tra ordinamento internazionale ed europeo. In L. Casini, ed., *La globalizzazione dei beni culturali* (pp. 171-196). Bologna: Il Mulino.

Yanes Cabrera, C. (2007). El patrimonio educativo intangible: Un recurso emergente en la museología educativa. *Cadernos de História da Educação* (2), 71-85.

Yanes Cabrera, C. (2008). Etnografia ed elementi "immateriali" della cultura scolastica: Possibilità e proposte di ricerca. In A. Gramigna & A. Ravaglia, eds., *Etnografia della formazione* (pp. 155-174). Roma: Anicia.

Yanes Cabrera, C. (2010). El patrimonio educativo inmaterial: propuestas para su recuperación y salvaguardia. In J. R. Berrio, ed., *El patrimonio histórico-educativo. Su conservación y estudio* (pp. 63-90). Madrid: Editorial Biblioteca Nueva.

Yanes Cabrera, C. (2011). The museum as a representation space of popular culture and educational memory. *History of Education & Children's Literature, 6* (2), 19-31.

Zago, G. (2015). L'insegnamento di storia della pedagogia nel magistero di Padova (1955-1980). In G. Zago, ed., *Sguardi storici sull'educazione dell'infanzia. Studi in onore di Mirella Chiaranda* (pp. 351-365). Fano: Aras Edizioni.

Zuccoli, F. (2010). *Dalle tasche dei bambini… Gli oggetti, le storie e la didattica.* Parma: Junior Edizioni.

Contributors

Anna Ascenzi is a Full Professor of History of Education and Children's Literature at the Department of Education, Cultural Heritage and Tourism of the University of Macerata (Italy). From 2010 to 2020 she was Director of the "Paolo & Ornella Ricca" Museum of the School, part of the same university. Since 2017, she has been appointed President of the Italian Society for Research on Historical-Educational Heritage (SIPSE).

Francesca Borruso is a Full Professor of History of Education at the Department of Education Sciences at the University of Roma Tre, where she teaches *History of childhood and pedagogy*, as well as *History of the school and educational institutions*. At the same university, she serves as Deputy Director of the "Mauro Laeng" Museum of the School and Education. She is a member of the SIPSE thematic Committee "Cataloguing of school heritage"

Marta Brunelli is an Associate Professor in General and Social Education at the Department of Education, Cultural Heritage and Tourism of the University of Macerata. As a researcher in *Heritage education*, since 2014 she has been the Head of educational service at the "Paolo & Ornella Ricca" Museum of school history, where she now serves as Deputy-Director. Since 2017, she has been a member of the SIPSE thematic Committee "Cataloguing of school heritage".

Mara Orlando is the former Curator of the Museum of Education at the University of Padua, where she was also responsible for the digital cataloguing of the school's artefacts between 2010 and 2021. Since 2017, she has been a member of the SIPSE thematic Commit-

tee "Cataloguing of school heritage" and a trainer of digital cataloguing of school heritage in SigecWeb.

Francesca Davida Pizzigoni is the Coordinator of SIPSE thematic
Committee "Cataloguing of school heritage". Since 2014 she has
been a Researcher at the INDIRE-National Institute of Educational
Documentation, Innovation and Research of the Ministry of education, and responsible for school heritage-based projects. Currently
she is Assistant-Professor (Researcher Type-B) in History of Education at the Department of Philosophy and Education Sciences of
the University of Turin.

Valeria Viola is an Assistant Professor (Researcher Type-A) in
History of Education at the "Giustino Fortunato" University, and
a member of the scientific Committee of the Museum of the School
and Popular Education at the University of Molise (Campobasso).
Since 2017, she has been a member of the SIPSE thematic Committee on "Cataloguing of school heritage.".

Carmen Vitale is an Assistant Professor (Senior Permanent
Researcher) in Administrative Law at the Department of Education, Cultural Heritage and Tourism of the University of Macerata
(Italy), where she researches and teaches *Administrative law and
cultural heritage* and *Tourism law* .